Read Reflect Respond

Comprehension Skill-Boosters

by **JOANNE SUTER**

Comprehension Skill-Boosters

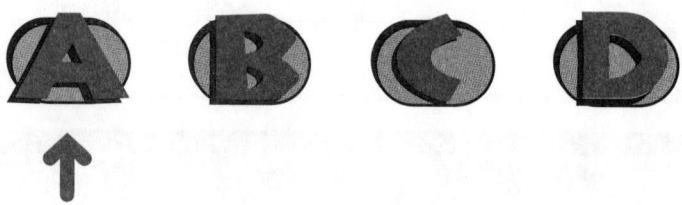

Development and Production: Laurel Associates, Inc.
Cover Design: Image Quest, Inc.

SADDLEBACK
EDUCATIONAL PUBLISHING
Three Watson
Irvine, CA 92618-2767
Website: www.sdlback.com

Copyright © 2006 by Saddleback Educational Publishing. All rights reserved. No part of this book may be reproduced in any form or by any means, electronic or mechanical, including photocopying, recording, or by any information storage and retrieval system, without the written permission of the publisher.

ISBN 1-59905-000-5

Printed in the United States of America
12 11 10 09 08 07 06   9 8 7 6 5 4 3 2 1

Read · Reflect · Respond
CONTENTS

A Note to the Student 5

LESSON 1: *Sharks Never Sleep* and Other Shark Facts 6

LESSON 2: Heroes from History: The Buffalo Soldiers 8

LESSON 3: Phew! What's That Smell? 10

LESSON 4: John Muir (1838–1914): Father of America's National Parks .12

LESSON 5: Camels and Their Humps 14

LESSON 6: The Ends of the Earth: The North and South Poles 16

LESSON 7: Meet Rosie the Riveter 18

LESSON 8: Through Rain, Snow, Sleet, and Hail 20

LESSON 9: *Would You Want to Buy One of These?*
Some Very Peculiar Patents 22

LESSON 10: How to Get a Passport 24

LESSON 11: The Truth About Dogs 26

LESSON 12: City Coyotes 28

LESSON 13: On the Bayou 30

LESSON 14: Happy Birthday, Pac-Man 32

LESSON 15: Rachael Scdoris 34

LESSON 16: Pumpkin Moon 36

LESSON 17: Cesar Chavez Fights for *La Causa* 38

LESSON 18: Writing a Business Letter 40

LESSON 19: Samurai Warriors 42

LESSON 20: How Animals Breathe 44

LESSON 21: Death Valley 46

LESSON 22: How to Ride a Bus . . . and More! 48

LESSON 23: The Trojan Horse 50

LESSON 24: Chimp Art 52

LESSON 25: Angels on Earth: Clara Barton and Florence Nightingale . . .54

LESSON 26: A Nutrition Update 56

LESSON 27: Words from History: *Give Me Liberty* 58

SUPER LESSON: The Oregon Trail 60

Read · Reflect · Respond

A NOTE TO THE STUDENT

How well do you understand and remember what you read? Can you count on your comprehension skills to meet the challenges of today's fast-paced world? The skill-sharpening exercises in the READ•REFLECT•RESPOND books can help you build confidence as you build competence.

The purpose of reading is to connect the ideas on the page to what you already know. That's why the short reading selections in these books work to your advantage. Each reading provides a clear mental framework for ideas and information. This makes it easier for you to grasp the main idea and sort out significant details. After you complete two or three lessons, you'll become familiar with the various kinds of responses required. This familiarity will alert you to important cues in the reading material. You'll learn to focus on key vocabulary, important facts, and the core message of the content. In short, you will become a more efficient reader.

We suggest that you thumb through each book before you begin the first lesson. Notice that the readings are engaging and informative—some are lighthearted and humorous, while others are more serious and thought-provoking. Glance at the question pages to see how they're organized. "Surveying" this book (or any book) in this informal way is called "prereading." It will help you "get a fix on" the task ahead.

Happy reading!

READ · REFLECT · RESPOND
LESSON 1

Read: *Do you know these interesting facts about sharks?*

SHARKS NEVER SLEEP AND OTHER SHARK FACTS

- **Sharks are ancient creatures.** They were around some 400 million years ago! Even before dinosaurs roamed the earth, sharks hunted the seas.

- **Sharks are survival machines.** They're well-designed to stay alive. They have the strongest jaws on the planet. Unlike other animals, both their upper and lower jaws move. If a shark loses a tooth, it's no problem. Why? Another tooth spins forward from a back-up row. In its lifetime, one shark may grow and use more than 20,000 teeth! Sharks can feed on nearly any creature in the sea. The only animals that see sharks as food are other sharks, whales, and human beings.

- **No bones about it!** Instead of bones, a shark's body has cartilage—hard, bendable stuff like the material in human ears. This makes the shark flexible. Tough shark "skin" has hard, razor-sharp scales.

- **Seven super senses!** Sharks have the same five senses humans do: sight, hearing, smell, taste, and touch. But there are differences. Two-thirds of a shark's brain is at work smelling things. It can smell one drop of blood in the sea. Humans use their noses for smelling and breathing, but a shark's nose is only for smell. Sharks see things in color. They can make out a light 10 times dimmer than any light we can see.

  And sharks have two bonus senses. A line of sensors from head to tail picks up vibrations. They can sense an injured fish quivering in the distance. Another sense lets sharks "feel" electricity. A shark can sense electric pulses from a beating heart.

- **Where's mama?** Unlike most animals, sharks don't take care of their babies. Newborn pups fend for themselves. In some species, the strongest pup eats its brothers and sisters. This improves its own chances of survival.

- **No need for a wake-up call!** Some types of sharks must swim constantly in order to breathe. Sharks go from periods of strong activity to times of calmer rest. But it is true that sharks are ever-watchful. They *never* sleep.

Reflect: *Think about sharks.*

1. Circle the four adjectives that describe sharks.

   flexible   watchful   motherly
   sleepy   ancient   vegetarian
   alert   soft   furry

2. Sometimes the word "shark" is used to describe a person. What traits might such a person have?

   _____
   _____
   _____

LESSON 1: *SHARKS NEVER SLEEP* AND OTHER SHARK FACTS

RESPOND: *Circle a letter or word, fill in the blanks, or write out the answer.*

Identify a main idea.

1. Which is a main idea of this reading?
   a. Sharks are well-equipped to survive.
   b. Sharks have lots of teeth.
   c. Sharks pups can be mean.

2. Write one *detail* from the reading that supports the *main idea* you selected.
   _____
   _____
   _____

Recall details.

3. Sharks have been around
   a. since the early 1900s.
   b. longer than dinosaurs.
   c. less time than human beings.

4. Besides the usual five senses, a shark can also sense
   a. weather and seasonal changes.
   b. outcomes of future events.
   c. vibrations and electricity.

5. When it comes to caring for their young, sharks
   a. are over-protective.
   b. ignore their offspring.
   c. teach their offspring hunting skills.

6. A baby shark is called a
   a. tadpole.   b. cub.   c. pup.

7. Sharks never
   a. give birth.   b. eat.   c. sleep.

Match synonyms.

8. ____ flexible   a. stay alive
9. ____ vibrations   b. alert
10. ____ survive   c. bendable
11. ____ watchful   d. quiverings

Make comparisons.

12. List three ways a shark body is different from a human body.
    • _____
    • _____
    • _____

Look it up in a reference source.

13. Name three species of shark.
    • _____
    • _____
    • _____

14. Are human swimmers usually in great danger from sharks? (Give details to explain and support your answer.)
    _____
    _____
    _____
    _____
    _____
    _____

LESSON 2

READ: *Learn about America's first black troops.*

HEROES FROM HISTORY: THE BUFFALO SOLDIERS

In 1888, some unusual American soldiers galloped their horses across the Great Plains. All of these men had dark hair and skin. They were known as the Buffalo Soldiers.

Earlier that century, many African-Americans had fought for the North in the Civil War. They'd helped to end slavery. After the war, in July of 1866, the army formed the 9th and 10th Cavalries. Each unit was made up entirely of African-American soldiers. White officers commanded these troops.

On the plains and in the southwest, Native Americans watched these soldiers carefully. They admired their courage in the face of danger. Like the buffalo that the Native Americans held sacred, these soldiers were dark, fierce, strong, and full of energy. That's why the Native Americans called these men "Buffalo Soldiers," a term of respect.

Many white troops and civilians looked down on the Buffalo Soldiers. But the all-black units performed well, even in the face of prejudice. The motto of the 9th Cavalry was *"We can! We will!"* The Buffalo Soldiers scouted dangerous regions. They battled hostile Native Americans and made peace with many tribes. They captured outlaws and mapped uncharted lands. They delivered mail, built telegraph lines, and protected forts, railroads, and wagon trains.

Several Buffalo Soldiers received Medals of Honor. The 9th and 10th Cavalries had fewer deserters than other army units. These brave men led the way for settlers and helped shape the West.

The story of the Buffalo Soldiers didn't end in the Wild West, however. All-black units served the U.S. armed forces into the 20th century. But not until 1992 were these troops honored officially. Since then, new monuments and movies have paid tribute to these heroes from America's history.

1994 BUFFALO SOLDIER COMMEMORATIVE STAMP

REFLECT: *Think about the Buffalo Soldiers and their role on the western frontier.*

1. Think about life on the American frontier. Then name two difficult or dangerous things about that life.

2. What, in your opinion, makes a person a hero?

LESSON 2: HEROES FROM HISTORY: THE BUFFALO SOLDIERS

3. What is the Medal of Honor? (Check a reference source for help.) Why might a soldier be awarded this medal?

_____
_____
_____

RESPOND: *Circle a letter or word, fill in the blanks, or write out the answer.*

Recall details.

1. How were the men of the 9th and 10th Cavalry different from soldiers of other army units?
   _____

2. What nickname did the Native Americans give the 9th and 10th Cavalry?
   _____

3. Why did the Native Americans give them that nickname?
   _____
   _____

4. What were three jobs done by the 9th and 10th Cavalry?
   - _____
   - _____
   - _____

5. What was the motto of the 9th Cavalry?
   _____

Recognize the author's purpose.

6. Why do you think the author wrote this article?
   a. to give credit to some of history's lesser-known heroes
   b. to create myths about life in the Old West
   c. to explain why the South lost the Civil War

Build your vocabulary.

7. *Cavalry* soldiers (rode horseback / traveled on foot).

8. The Native Americans thought the buffalo were *sacred* or (scarce / holy).

9. The Native Americans *respected* or (admired / disliked) the Buffalo Soldiers.

10. The Buffalo Soldiers fought against *hostile* or (friendly / unfriendly) Native Americans.

11. Many white soldiers (admired / looked down on) the black soldiers because of *prejudice*.

12. Because very few black soldiers (ran away from their duties / were paid for their work), the 9th and 10th Cavalries had few *deserters*.

Look it up in a reference source.

13. Cathay Williams was the only female to serve as a Buffalo Soldier. Do some research about her. Then write a few sentences telling her story.
    _____
    _____
    _____
    _____
    _____
    _____

LESSON 3

READ: *Learn more about your sense of smell—one of the five human senses.*

PHEW! WHAT'S THAT SMELL?

You open the refrigerator door. *Phew!* What's that awful odor? Your sense of smell is warning you that food has spoiled!

The human sense of smell is very sensitive. It is not, however, as highly developed in humans as in most animals. Many animals use their sense of smell as their first line of protection. Their nose tells them when an enemy is near. And it leads them to food.

Smells come to us as very tiny particles in the air called *molecules*. When you breathe, the molecules go into your nose. Take a moment. Sniff the air. Breathe in those molecules! What odors do you smell?

The human nose has two holes called *nostrils*. Inside each nostril are nerve cells. They pick up the odor first. Then they pass it to the *olfactory* nerve, which leads to the brain. At that moment we smell the smell!

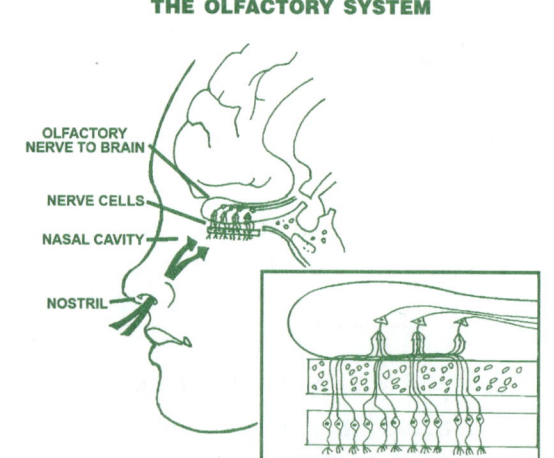

THE OLFACTORY SYSTEM

THREE FACTS ABOUT THE SENSE OF SMELL

- The olfactory lobes take up more of an animal's brain than a human's.
- A specific odor may seem strong when we first sense it. After about three minutes, though, we usually stop smelling it.
- Many "tastes" are really blends of smells and tastes. Is it an onion or an apple? If you hold your nose after taking a bite, it's hard to tell.

REFLECT: *Think about different smells.*

1. Name an aroma, such as that of strawberries, that reminds you of something *pleasant*. _____

2. Name an odor that reminds you of something *unpleasant*. _____

3. Certain smells can warn of danger. List three smells that may mean that danger is near.

   _____ _____ _____

4. Sniff the air. List some of the odors you smell. _____

   _____

5. After a few minutes, you usually stop noticing an odor. How might that be a good thing? How might that be bad?

_____
_____
_____
_____

RESPOND: Circle a letter or word, fill in the blanks, or write out the answer.

Build your vocabulary.

1. The air is filled with _m_____ that carry odor.

2. You breathe odors in through the _n_____ in your nose.

3. The _o_____ nerve carries the smell to the _b_____.

Think about parts and wholes.

4. Many parts of your body work together to make your sense of smell work. List three main parts of your whole "smelling system."

_____
_____
_____

Recall details.

5. Human beings have a (stronger / weaker) sense of smell than most animals.

6. We normally stop smelling a specific odor after experiencing it for several (minutes / hours).

7. Strong odors can affect what we (taste / see).

8. Your food might have a different taste if you (closed your eyes / plugged your nose).

Put details in order.

9. The following sentences describe how your sense of smell works. Number them in the order in which they happen.

    ____ a. The odor is carried to your brain.

    ____ b. You breathe in odor molecules.

    ____ c. Odor molecules fill the air.

    ____ d. Nerve cells sense the odor.

Look it up in a reference source.

10. Where is an insect's sense organ for smell?

    _____

11. *Anosmia* is an olfactory disorder. What is the primary symptom of this disorder?

    _____

READ • REFLECT • RESPOND
LESSON 4

READ: *Learn about a man who loved and protected our natural resources.*

JOHN MUIR (1838–1914): FATHER OF AMERICA'S NATIONAL PARKS

John Muir was a student of nature. As a boy he had little schooling, yet he later became an author. He wrote that a day in the mountains was ". . . better than a cartload of books."

At age 11, John came to the United States from Scotland. His family settled on a Midwestern farm. Hard work filled his days, but John made time to read and explore. And he also found time to invent. Among other things, he invented an automatic horse feeder.

As a young man, he studied at the University of Wisconsin. After college, Muir traveled. Along the way, a factory job ended in an accident that nearly blinded him. When his eyesight returned, he vowed to treasure nature's brightness. That's when Muir set off on a 1,000-mile walk from Indiana to Florida. After that he went on to Cuba and Panama. Finally, he settled in California. Muir spent many happy years living in the mountains there. He wrote that he often stood atop a waterfall and sang out with joy.

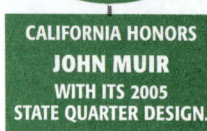

CALIFORNIA HONORS **JOHN MUIR** WITH ITS 2005 STATE QUARTER DESIGN.

John Muir made it his full-time job to write and speak about the glories of nature. His works helped convince U.S. President Theodore Roosevelt to protect the California wilderness. The president even joined Muir on a camping trip. That inspired him to set aside land as Yosemite National Park and Sequoia National Park.

John Muir became the first president of the Sierra Club. To this day, the club's mission is to protect natural beauty for everyone to enjoy.

California has showed its gratitude to Muir many times. There are more California sites named after John Muir than after any other person!

Muir sent his messages from the peaks of the Sierra Nevada range, the shade of Sequoia trees, beneath the stars, and beside riverbeds. He gave all Americans some good advice: "Keep close to Nature's heart . . . Break clear away, once in awhile. Climb a mountain or spend a week in a forestland. Wash your spirit clean!"

REFLECT: *Think about John Muir and the beauty of nature.*

1. Circle the places that are "natural" regions.

a mountain meadow	a new shopping mall	a dry desert	a deep valley
Kennedy Airport	a sparkling waterfall	a college campus	a dark forest
the Grand Canyon	the Florida Everglades	a city library	Central Park

LESSON 4: JOHN MUIR (1838–1914): FATHER OF AMERICA'S NATIONAL PARKS

2. Is there a special place of natural beauty that you enjoy? Tell about it.
_____
_____

3. Why do you think John Muir has been called the "Father of America's National Parks"?
_____
_____

4. Think about the quote at the end of the passage. Rewrite the quotation in your own words.
_____
_____

RESPOND: Circle a letter or word, fill in the blanks, or write out the answer.

Build your vocabulary.

1. Combine a word from Box A with a word from Box B to make a *compound word* from the reading. Then use that word to complete each sentence.

BOX A	BOX B
water eye	bed land
river forest	fall sight

   a. A stream or river that spills over the top of a cliff and pours to the ground is a _____.

   b. A _____ is the area between the banks of a waterway covered or once covered by water.

   c. A large wooded area can be called a _____.

   d. Another word for *vision* is _____.

Recall details.

2. John Muir came to America from
   a. Italy.   b. Ireland   c. Scotland.

3. When he was young, Muir loved to
   a. paint nature pictures.
   b. invent unusual things.
   c. take care of animals.

4. Muir wrote articles about
   a. protecting nature.
   b. scientific discoveries.
   c. life in the Midwest.

Look it up in a reference source.

5. Write three facts about the Sierra Club.
   • _____
   • _____
   • _____

READ·REFLECT·RESPOND
LESSON 5

READ: Why are camels sometimes called "ships of the desert"?

TITLE: _____

Dry winds blow sand as a train of camels trudges across the vast desert. The desert people depend on camels. These remarkable beasts serve as pack animals on long, hot journeys. Desert travelers pack their gear against the hump on a camel's back. This hump is the camel's most distinct feature. Camels are, in fact, the *only* animals with humps. People often think the hump is filled with water. But it is not a storage depot for liquid. Actually, it's a mound of fat.

The fat mound helps the camel survive on desert crossings. A camel's hump can weigh up to 80 pounds. When food or water becomes scarce, the camel's body draws on the reserves of fat in its hump. This allows the camel to survive for weeks without eating or drinking.

As the camel's body uses the fat, the hump shrinks. Eventually, it may get so empty and small that it flops onto the camel's side! The size of the hump is a sign of the camel's health. A camel-rancher explained, "It's time to worry when a hump starts to tip. That means the animal needs food!" Once a camel gets food and water, its hump returns to normal. And as for food, a camel will eat just about anything! A very hungry camel will eat tents, ropes, or even saddle straps! Grasses and grains are more healthful, of course.

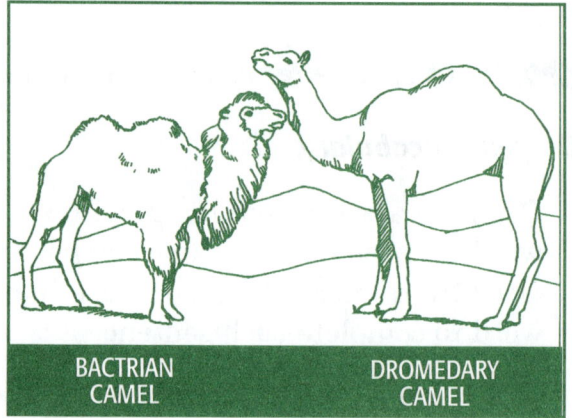
BACTRIAN CAMEL   DROMEDARY CAMEL

The most commonly seen camels have one hump. These are the desert-dwellers of Africa and Arabia. Two-humped camels are found mainly in the deserts of Asia. They are shorter and heavier than one-humped camels. Their long, thick hair helps them withstand the region's great heat and extreme cold.

REFLECT: *Think about camels.*

1. Circle the title that would best fit this article. Then write the title above the reading.

   The Dry Desert Lands   *Hey, Mr. Camel! What's in That Hump?*   *The Daily Life of a Camel*

2. Explain why you chose that title. _____

_____

LESSON 5: (to be titled by student)

3. Write the names of three other "pack animals."

   _____
   _____
   _____

4. Describe a place where camels live. Circle three descriptive adjectives.

   dry   sandy   wooded

   hot   damp   seaside

RESPOND: Circle a letter or word, fill in the blanks, or write out the answer.

Build your vocabulary.

1. A camel's hump is its most *distinct* feature. The word *distinct* means

   a. noticeable   b. ugly   c. useful

2. The camel's hump is a *depot*. A *depot* is a kind of

   a. storehouse.   b. tumor.   c. sore spot.

3. A camel's hump helps it *survive*. To *survive* is to

   a. run.   b. see well.   c. stay alive.

4. The camel is a desert *dweller*. The word *dweller* means

   a. traveler.   b. animal.   c. resident.

5. The deserts of Asia have *extreme* heat and cold. *Extreme* means

   a. slight.   b. very great.   c. moist.

Identify the main idea.

6. This reading is mainly about
   a. different types of camels.
   b. the camel's hump.
   c. the different places that camels live.

Recall details.

7. As the camel uses up stored fat, its hump (grows / shrinks).

8. A very large hump may weigh (eight / eighty) pounds.

9. A camel with a very small, floppy hump is probably (hungry / young).

10. Camels can go for weeks without (food / sleep).

11. Camels are (picky / greedy) eaters.

12. The most commonly seen camels have (one hump / two humps).

Look it up in a reference source.

13. How does a camel keep desert sand out of its nose?

    _____
    _____

14. What protects a camel's eyes from the blowing sand?

    _____
    _____
    _____
    _____
    _____
    _____

LESSON 6

READ: *How is the North Pole different from the South Pole?*

THE ENDS OF THE EARTH: THE NORTH AND SOUTH POLES

Travel as far north as possible, and you will reach the North Pole. Nothing is north of the North Pole. Travel as far south as possible, and you'll reach the South Pole. Nothing is south of the South Pole. Found on opposite ends of the world, the poles have some very different features.

The Arctic Ocean covers the region that includes the North Pole. There is no land beneath the thick polar ice cap. Unlike the North Pole, the South Pole is solid land. In fact, it is part of the continent of Antarctica.

Seasons come at opposite times at the poles. Average July temperatures at the North Pole rise to 32°F. In February, temperatures plunge to -31°F. But the South Pole gets much colder! The average annual temperature there is -52°F. Winter lows have hit -117°F. Why is the North Pole warmer than the South Pole? The North Pole sits over water that never freezes solid. Ocean currents warm the region from below the surface. At both poles, winter brings six months of nighttime. The dark months have their own special beauty. Stars shine 24 hours a day.

Penguins, seals, and sea birds live along Antarctica's coasts. But there's no animal life at the South Pole itself. Because this pole is inland and high, the climate is simply too cold! Polar bears, walruses, and whales inhabit the Arctic region. But there are no penguins! Penguins are found only in the southern half of the world.

REFLECT: *Think about the North and South Poles.*

1. Circle the four adjectives that describe both the North and South Poles.

   | hot | frozen | tropical | fertile |
   | cold | empty | crowded | barren |

2. Which pole is closer to Canada?

3. Which pole is closer to Australia?

4. What is the coldest place you've ever visited? How cold was it? How was daily life different in the cold?

LESSON 6: THE ENDS OF THE EARTH: THE NORTH AND SOUTH POLES

RESPOND: Circle a letter or word, fill in the blanks, or write out the answer.

Recall details.

1. The North Pole is really (a land mass / an ice cap).

2. Because it is so cold at the South Pole, there is no (summer / animal life).

3. Both poles are (dark / cold) six months a year.

Make comparisons.

4. List two ways the North Pole and South Pole are alike.

   • _____

   • _____

5. List two ways the North Pole and South Pole are different.

   • _____

   • _____

Draw conclusions.

6. Explain why Arctic polar bears don't eat penguins.

   _____
   _____
   _____
   _____

Build your vocabulary.

7. The South Pole is on the *continent* of Antarctica. A *continent* is
   a. a large country or nation.
   b. a network of waterways and land masses.
   c. one of the seven main, large land areas on the earth.

8. Ocean *currents* warm the North Pole. A *current* is
   a. a flow of water or air in a certain direction.
   b. a fish, sea lion, or walrus.
   c. an iceberg.

9. Both poles have a cold *climate*. *Climate* is the
   a. type of animal life found in a place.
   b. usual weather conditions in a place.
   c. storage building on a site.

10. Penguins *inhabit* Antarctica. To *inhabit* a place is to
    a. live there.
    b. die there.
    c. be born there.

Look it up in a dictionary.

11. The English word *pole* comes from what language? _____

    How was the word spelled in that language? _____

READ • REFLECT • RESPOND 17

READ • REFLECT • RESPOND
LESSON 7

READ: *What important step forward did women take during World War II?*

MEET ROSIE THE RIVETER

When the United States joined World War II, all of the nation's factories were "men-only" workplaces. Then American men were called to duty as soldiers. Who would make the goods needed by a country at war? Meet Rosie the Riveter!

Between 1942 and 1944, the U.S. government urged working women to leave traditional jobs such as store clerks and secretaries. It also called for homemakers to join the work force. It promised good wages and new skills. Rosie the Riveter became the symbol of the government's campaign. This fictional factory worker appeared in magazines, posters, and films. She wore a red bandanna and blue coveralls. Her rolled-up sleeve showed a strong arm. Her eyes were fiery. Her jaw was firm. The slogan "We Can Do It" blazed above her head. It dared women to join the fight. Rosie had muscles, but she was still glamorous. She was never shown without makeup!

The campaign was a big success. During WWII, the number of female workers grew by 50 percent. Women worked in mills, factories, and shipyards. They operated heavy machinery, unloaded freight, and built weapons. And they earned more than ever before!

Then the war ended and soldiers returned to their jobs. Even so, the role of women had changed. The number of women in the workforce never again fell as low as before WWII. Wartime "Rosies" now felt a new sense of pride and independence. After all, they had helped win the war!

REFLECT: *Think about WWII and the character called Rosie the Riveter.*

1. Why would a government ask women to work during wartime?

2. Look at the picture of Rosie the Riveter. Why do you think she is flexing her muscle?

LESSON 7: Meet Rosie the Riveter

3. After the war, do you think it was fair for men to reclaim the jobs women had been doing? Explain why or why not.

_____
_____
_____
_____

RESPOND: *Circle a letter or word, fill in the blanks, or write out the answer.*

Recall details.

1. Which factors drew women into WWII factories?
   a. patriotism
   b. higher pay
   c. chance to learn new skills
   d. all of the above

2. Who was Rosie the Riveter?
   a. a female soldier
   b. a WWII nurse
   c. a campaign symbol

3. Which slogan was part of the "Rosie" campaign?
   a. It's all in a day's work!
   b. We can do it!
   c. Victory now!

Build your vocabulary.

4. A *rivet* is a (metal bolt / airplane pilot).

5. A *campaign* is a (factory machine / crusade to accomplish something).

6. A *slogan* is a (catchy saying / type of weapon).

7. *Patriotism* is a love of (country / money).

8. A *bandanna* is a (shoe / scarf).

Identify a main idea.

9. Which is a *main idea* of this reading?
   a. Rosie the Riveter wore a head scarf and makeup.
   b. Rosie the Riveter was a symbol used to recruit women workers.
   c. World War II gave women a chance to make more money.

Look it up in a reference source.

10. Which countries were America's enemies in World War II?
    _____
    _____

11. America fought on the side of what other nations?
    _____
    _____

12. Who were the Nazis?
    _____
    _____
    _____

13. When and where did America use the atomic bomb?
    _____
    _____
    _____

READ · REFLECT · RESPOND
LESSON 8

READ: Compare four types of moisture that fall from the sky.

THROUGH RAIN, SNOW, SLEET, AND HAIL . . .

The U.S. Postal Service promises to deliver mail through rain, snow, sleet, and hail. That means you'll get your mail no matter what the weather is like! But what, exactly, are rain, snow, sleet, and hail?

Water from the clouds is called *precipitation*. When clouds become heavy, raindrops fall. Large raindrops fall faster than small ones.

When the temperature plunges below 32 degrees, precipitation freezes. Then moisture falls as sleet, hail, or snow. Some drops begin as rain but pass through cold air closer to the earth. These drops freeze when they hit an object such as dust in the air or a power line. Then precipitation turns into tiny white pellets called *sleet*. Sleet can make roads slippery and dangerous.

Sometimes rain falls through layers of cold and warm air. High, cold air freezes

SNOWFLAKES COME IN MANY SHAPES AND SIZES, BUT EVERY SNOWFLAKE HAS SIX SIDES.

the drops. As the frozen drops hit lower, warmer air, water collects around them. Then strong air currents pull them skyward, where the water freezes again. Winds may carry drops of hail, called *hailstones*, up and down many times. As they grow, the hailstones become too heavy to float, so they fall. Hail melts much more quickly than sleet.

Unlike sleet or hail, snow is already frozen when it leaves the clouds. What happens if the temperature near the earth is above freezing? Snow will turn to rain. But snowflakes fall if the air near earth stays at or below freezing.

REFLECT: Think about the weather in your region.

1. Circle four forms of moisture that can fall from the sky.

   rain   heat

   sleet   cold

   hail   snow

   clouds   wind

2. What kind of moisture is most common where you live?

   _____

   Why do you think that is the case? (Hint: In what region of the United States do you live?)

   _____
   _____
   _____

3. Name a place where . . .

   it often snows.

   _____

   it never snows.

   _____

   it seldom rains.

   _____

LESSON 8: THROUGH RAIN, SNOW, SLEET, AND HAIL...

RESPOND: Circle a letter or word, fill in the blank, or write out the answer.

Make comparisons.

1. How is rain different from other forms of precipitation?
   a. It is frozen.
   b. It is not frozen.
   c. It is not as wet.

2. Which raindrops fall fastest?
   a. big ones
   b. frozen ones
   c. small ones

3. How is snow different from sleet and hail?
   a. It falls to the ground.
   b. It freezes in the air.
   c. It forms in the clouds.

4. Why is hail less dangerous than sleet?
   a. It is softer.
   b. It melts faster.
   c. It never reaches the ground.

Build your vocabulary.

5. *Precipitation* is
   a. water from the clouds.
   b. very cold weather.
   c. frozen ground.

6. The *temperature* is
   a. the amount of moisture in the air.
   b. the measure of warmth or cold.
   c. the strength of the wind.

7. A *hailstone* is
   a. an ice-coated rock.
   b. a very hard snowball.
   c. a ball of frozen precipitation.

Draw conclusions.

8. A spring thunderstorm is under way. Precipitation passes through layers of cold and warm air. This precipitation is likely to fall as

   _____.

9. The temperature near the ground is very, very cold. Rain falls from the clouds and passes through freezing air layers. This precipitation hits the ground as

   _____.

10. Grab your umbrella! The air is quite warm, but there are heavy, dark clouds overhead. _____ is likely to fall.

11. It's freezing cold up high in the air and down low near the ground! Precipitation coming out of the clouds will fall as

    _____.

READ•REFLECT•RESPOND 21

READ · REFLECT · RESPOND
LESSON 9

READ: *Necessity is the mother of invention. Or is it?*

WOULD YOU WANT TO BUY ONE OF THESE? SOME VERY PECULIAR PATENTS

A *patent* is an official permit issued by the government. It grants people or companies special rights. It says that they can be the only ones to make or sell a new invention. A patent protects an idea from copycats. Most products we use—from the yo-yo to the dishwasher—are protected by patents. Other patented products are much less familiar.

In the 1990s, an American invented the *toe puppet*. Its patent protects the design for a "puppet to be mounted on a single human toe. . . . The movement of the toe causes the figure to move to and fro." Now that's an unusual form of fun!

You've probably never heard of the *gravity-powered shoe air conditioner*. It's a tiny heating and cooling system built into the heel of a shoe. How is the device powered? By the pressure created from walking. This inventor was apparently quite an engineer!

And how about the *ear protector for long-eared dogs*? According to the inventor, these special tubes "contain and protect the dog's ears. The tubes hold the ears away from the dog's mouth and food as it eats."

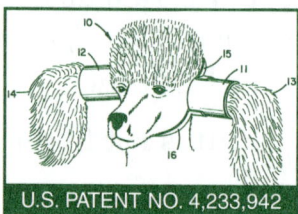

Bird owners may also appreciate the inventor of the *bird diaper*. (Its purpose needs no explanation.)

Parents might want to invest in the *portable automobile partition*. It's a see-through divider designed to separate children in the backseat and prevent fighting. If that's not enough, a deluxe, solid-color model prevents kids from making faces at each other.

What would *you* like to patent? Put on your own thinking cap. You might come up with a brainchild of your own!

REFLECT: *Think about inventors and their inventions.*

1. Look around the room. Name an important or useful invention you can see. (A computer would be an example.) Tell why you chose this invention.

   _____
   _____
   _____

2. Complete the following sentence:
   I'd like to invent a device that would
   _____
   _____

LESSON 9: WOULD YOU WANT TO BUY ONE OF THESE? SOME VERY PECULIAR PATENTS

3. Which invention mentioned in the reading sounded like a fairly good idea? Which one sounded like a very silly idea? Explain your choices.

GOOD IDEA: _____   SILLY IDEA: _____

_____   _____

_____   _____

_____   _____

RESPOND: Circle a letter or word, fill in the blanks, or write out the answer.

Recall details.

1. What is a patent?
   a. an invention
   b. an official document
   c. an inventor

2. What is the purpose of a patent?
   a. to protect an inventor's idea
   b. to advertise a new product
   c. to help an inventor design a new product

3. Who issues a patent?
   a. the inventor
   b. a store
   c. the government

4. What is the purpose of the gravity-powered shoe air conditioner?
   a. to heat a cold shoe
   b. to cool a hot shoe
   c. to both heat and cool a shoe

5. Who would most likely purchase the portable automobile partition?
   a. an animal lover
   b. a parent
   c. a jogger

Recognize the author's tone.

6. The *tone* of this reading is
   a. informal, light, and friendly.
   b. formal and serious.
   c. scientific and scholarly.

Build your vocabulary.

7. *A patent protects an idea from copycats.*
   In that sentence, the word *patent* is used as a (noun / verb).

8. *Someone patented the yo-yo.*
   In that sentence, the word *patented* is used as a (noun / verb).

Look it up in a dictionary.

9. A *copycat* is someone who _____ _____.

10. *Gravity* is _____ _____ _____.

11. The purpose of a *partition* is to _____ _____.

12. The meaning of *brainchild* is _____ _____.

READ·REFLECT·RESPOND 23

READ·REFLECT·RESPOND
LESSON 10

READ: Planning an out-of-country trip? Here's how!

HOW TO GET A PASSPORT

Christina will soon travel to Brazil. Because she's going out of the United States, she needs a passport. This official travel document is recognized around the world. In foreign countries, it will prove that Christina is who she says she is. It will show that she comes from the United States. Only the U.S. Department of State can issue a United States passport.

First, Christina turns to the Internet. She types in the address of the official passport website: *travel.state.gov/passport*. There she finds instructions on how to get her passport.

Christina finds out that she must apply in person because she's never had a U.S. passport. Many post offices and public libraries accept applications and issue passports.

Christina prints out an application from the computer website. Now she can fill out the two-page form (number DS-11) at home. But she must sign the form in front of the passport agent.

Christina goes to the main branch of her city post office. Along with the completed application, she must show proof of U.S. citizenship. She brings her birth certificate and driver's license. Christina also gives her Social Security number, although that alone does not serve as identification. The website lists other ID options.

Next, Christina gets two passport photos.

Finally, Christina pays the fees. Then she will wait about six weeks to receive her passport. That's why she applied for her passport three months before her trip. She knows she needs the document in hand before she sets off!

REFLECT: Consider what you know about passports.

1. What is the purpose of a passport? _____

2. Why do you think most countries require a passport for foreign travel? _____

3. Do you have a passport? _____

4. Do you think it's a good idea to require a photo on the passport? Explain your answer. _____

LESSON 10: HOW TO GET A PASSPORT

RESPOND: *Circle a letter or word, fill in the blanks, or write out the answer.*

Recall details.

1. Circle four items a person must provide to get a passport.

   application form   a travel plan

   education history   identification

   proof of employment   recent photo

   proof of citizenship   medical records

   three character references

Put details in order.

2. To get her passport, what was the *first* step Christina took?
   a. She went online and checked a website.
   b. She paid a modest fee.
   c. She signed the application.

3. When did Christina fill out the passport application?
   a. before she went to the post office
   b. when she reached the post office
   c. at home after returning from the post office

4. What was the *last* thing Christina did at the passport office?
   a. She planned her trip to Brazil.
   b. She received her passport.
   c. She paid the fee.

Build your vocabulary.

5. An official paper, such as a birth certificate or passport, can be called a (*document* / *pamphlet*).

6. As used in this reading, the abbreviation *U.S.* stands for (Under Suspicion / United States).

7. The abbreviation *ID* stands for (identification / Internet data).

8. The number DS-11 represents the passport (application form / office address).

Draw a conclusion.

9. According to the reading, how long does it usually take to get a passport?
   _____

10. Why do you think Christina applied for her passport three full months before her trip?
    _____
    _____
    _____
    _____

Look it up in a reference source.

11. Suppose an applicant doesn't have a driver's license. What other forms of identification are acceptable?
    _____
    _____

12. What are the guidelines for a passport photo?
    _____
    _____

13. What is the current charge for a passport? _____

READ·REFLECT·RESPOND   25

LESSON 11

READ: Compare "fact vs. fiction" as you read about dogs.

THE TRUTH ABOUT DOGS

- **MYTH:** *One dog year equals seven human years.*

    Dogs *do* age much faster than people. But there's no exact formula to compare aging. Experts believe that a dog's first year equals about 16 human years. Think about it: In just one year, a dog becomes a teenager! Then the seven-year theory goes into effect for awhile. By age two, typical dogs compare to humans in their twenties. By age 3, a pup is pushing 30.

    A dog's size and breed affects its aging. Samson, a St. Bernard, ages faster than Bitsy, a toy poodle. A 10-year-old dog of a giant breed is roughly equivalent to a 78-year-old human. In contrast, a 10-year-old dog of a small breed may be as lively as a 56-year-old.

- **MYTH:** *Dogs are color-blind.*

    It's true that dogs don't see colors just as people do. For example, green may look more like yellow to a dog. But dogs don't live in a world of gray. Some experts believe that dogs see certain shades of blue and purple even more clearly than people do. Do you need proof? A husky named Sitka loved the mail carrier who carried biscuits along with mail. Whenever Sitka met someone wearing "Postal Service" blue, she wildly begged for treats.

- **MYTH:** *A dog's mouth is cleaner than a human's.*

    Dog saliva does indeed kill some germs. A pup, however, has its own unique "doggy germs." These could be a danger—especially to little children or elderly people.

- **MYTH:** *It's cruel to keep a dog inside when you're away. Dogs prefer to be left outside to play.*

    Indoor dogs think of the house as their den. They feel safe inside. Many pups will bark and dig if they're left outside too long. When they're alone for many hours, most dogs prefer a cozy nest to the great outdoors.

REFLECT: Think about the dogs you know.

1. Name three breeds of very large dogs.
    - _____
    - _____
    - _____

   Name three breeds of very small dogs.
    - _____
    - _____
    - _____

2. Answer the following questions about a dog you know.

　•About how old is the dog? _____

　•Describe the dog's appearance. What color, size, and shape is it?
　_____
　_____

　•In human years, about how old is the dog? _____

3. Some people claim that dogs understand human language. Do you think that's true or a myth? Give reasons for your answer.
_____
_____
_____

RESPOND: Circle a letter or word, fill in the blanks, or write out the answer.

Build your vocabulary.

1. A m_ _ _ is a tale told over and over again for many years.

2. A poodle is a type of dog. A Siamese is a type of cat. An animal's type is its b_ _ _ _ _ .

3. A g_ _ _ is a tiny living thing that causes disease. It can only be seen through a microscope.

4. A wild animal, such as a bear or wolf, makes its home in a d_ _ .

5. To make a high-pitched, complaining cry is to w_ _ _ _ .

Recall details: True or False?

6. ____ One dog year always equals exactly seven human years.

7. ____ Dogs may see certain colors more clearly than human beings do.

8. ____ Dogs cannot see the color blue.

9. ____ A dog's mouth is germ-free.

10. ____ Dogs have some germs that are different than human germs.

11. ____ Dogs always prefer the outdoors to the indoors.

Recognize examples.

12. What example does the author use to prove that dogs can see colors?
_____
_____
_____
_____

Look it up in a reference source.

13. Name three *wild* members of the dog family.
_____
_____
_____

14. Name a breed of dog that is . . .

　a *terrier*. _____

　a *hound*. _____

READ·REFLECT·RESPOND
LESSON 12

READ: *What nonhumans are sharing your neighborhood?*

CITY COYOTES

There were strangers on our block. Neighbors had spotted a pair of coyotes in the brushy vacant lot. Then the animals appeared in some backyards. They were so bold as to stroll down the street at twilight. Now we've learned that our neighborhood's wildlife is not unusual. Once, coyotes lived only on the plains and deserts of the West. Now they inhabit every state except Hawaii. Coyotes have even roamed New York's Central Park. Across the country, neighborhoods are reporting "coyote invasions."

Actually, it's usually not the coyotes who are invaders. In most cases, these animals haven't moved into our neighborhoods. We've moved into theirs! Homes have been built in areas that were recently wild—and coyotes have adapted. When humans move in, the coyotes don't just leave. As long as they can find food, they stay around.

My neighbors worried about these creatures in our midst. Coyotes may look much like dogs. But they're not dogs—they're wild animals. We learned that the worst thing to do is to feed coyotes. So we got rid of all food sources. We removed garbage and pet food from our yards. We cleaned up drippings from barbecue grills. A coyote's natural diet includes rodents, rabbits, snakes, and berries. This animal will, however, be happy to try a new dish.

Pet owners had to be careful. Coyotes see cats and small dogs as prey. We human beings were cautious, too. Most coyotes will avoid people. Waving sticks, clanging pots, and making other loud noises usually scares them off. Even so, as they get used to people, they become bolder. Coyotes often lose their fear of us when we feed them. When the animals connect people with food, they may become fierce.

My neighbors and I learned to make our neighborhood less "coyote-friendly." We took away food and water sources. We cut back sheltering brush. It worked. Now the coyotes have found a new home!

REFLECT: *Think about coyotes and other wild animals sharing spaces with people.*

1. Make a list of wild animals you've seen in your neighborhood. (Hint: The list can include squirrels, opossums, etc.)

___

___

LESSON 12: CITY COYOTES

2. List two good things and two bad things about having wildlife in your own backyard.

   GOOD THINGS:
   • _____
   • _____

   BAD THINGS:
   • _____
   • _____

RESPOND: *Circle a letter or word, fill in the blanks, or write out the answer.*

Recall details.

1. Where in the United States are coyotes found today?
   a. from coast to coast
   b. only on the Great Plains
   c. mostly in urban areas

2. What's the best way to make sure coyotes hang around your neighborhood?
   a. make loud noises
   b. leave lights on at night
   c. feed them

3. Who has the most to fear from coyotes?
   a. human beings
   b. cats and small dogs
   c. the narrator

Recognize the main idea.

4. What is the main idea of this reading?
   a. Coyotes are dangerous when fed.
   b. Coyotes are sharing spaces with human beings.
   c. It's important to keep a clean yard.

Build your vocabulary.

| adaptable   cautious   invader   prey   sheltering |

5. An _____ is someone or something that comes into an area where it's not wanted.

6. To be _____ means to be well able to get along as things change.

7. To be careful is to be _____.

8. An animal that is hunted for food is called _____.

9. Something is _____ if it offers protection from weather and danger.

Draw conclusions.

10. In which types of areas would coyotes be most likely to appear? (Circle three.)

    a new suburb built in a wooded area
    a large, green city park
    a clean, well-kept yard
    a downtown with skyscrapers
    an amusement park
    a brushy, garbage-strewn yard

Look it up in a reference source.

11. Write three facts about coyotes that are not mentioned in the reading.
    • _____
    • _____
    • _____

READ•REFLECT•RESPOND

LESSON 13

READ: Alligators, snakes, and nutria . . . Oh, my!

ON THE BAYOU

Would you like to tour the Louisiana swamps? Use a flat-bottomed boat to travel the bayous. These slow-moving waterways wind through the low-lying areas of the Mississippi River delta.

The word *bayou* (say BYE-oo) was first used by the French in Louisiana. It comes from the Choctaw word *bayuk*, which means "small stream."

As you glide through the shady swampland, you'll find a world of eerie beauty. Spanish moss dangles like tinsel from the branches of live oaks and cypress trees. The dark, still surface mirrors the hanging wisps. According to one old story, these strands are hairs from the beard of a villain named Gorez Goz. The legend says that Goz tried to capture a lovely bayou maiden—but she was able to escape.

The Louisiana bayou teems with life. As the boat intrudes, you might see a heron perched on a fallen cypress branch, bald eagles soaring above, and some red-winged blackbirds singing in the trees. Perhaps you'll see a nutria darting from the shore to water. This hardy creature looks like a cross between a beaver and a rat. You'll see reptiles, too. Turtles paddle about. More than 100 kinds of snakes live in the swamp. Three types, including the cottonmouth, are poisonous. But the king of the bayou is the alligator. This fellow might look like a floating log—until its eyes and nose clear the surface. He splashes his scaly tail. The 'gator slides through the water and climbs onto the shore. He stretches out there to soak up sun.

It's usually hot on the bayou. The air is moist and heavy. If you're lucky, a breeze off the water will keep you cool enough to enjoy your journey. At dusk, the setting sun turns the dark waters a brilliant red-orange. When the moon rises, the Spanish moss takes on a mysterious glow. As you leave the bayou, the slender strands of moss seem to wave a ghostly farewell.

REFLECT: Think about what you'd see in a swamp.

1. Write three words you think of when you hear the word *bayou*.
   - _____
   - _____
   - _____

2. Would you enjoy taking a swamp tour? Explain why or why not.
   _____
   _____
   _____
   _____

LESSON 13: ON THE BAYOU

3. Describe a waterway you have seen. Tell something about its location, wildlife, climate, and surroundings.

_____
_____
_____

RESPOND: Circle a letter or word, fill in the blanks, or write out the answer.

Recall details.

1. What is the history of the word *bayou*?
    a. a Native American word meaning "small stream"
    b. a Native American word meaning "alligator snout"
    c. a Canadian word meaning "travel south"

2. What wildlife could you expect to find on the bayou?
    a. trout, Canada geese, and foxes
    b. polar bears, penguins, and seals
    c. turtles, snakes, and birds

3. What plants would you be likely to find on the bayou?
    a. fir trees, pines, and tulips
    b. cypress trees, live oaks, and Spanish moss
    c. cacti, sagebrush, and junipers

4. What is the usual climate on the bayou?
    a. hot and dry
    b. hot and moist
    c. cold and icy

Make comparisons.

5. The bayou is most like a: (Circle one.)

    rapid river   irrigation system   ocean
    waterfall   slow-moving stream   pond

Build your vocabulary.

| delta | legend | reptile | swamp |

6. A _____ is a triangle-shaped piece of land. It's formed when sand and soil build up at the mouth of a large river.

7. A _____ is a tale that has been told for ages.

8. A _____, or marsh, is a wet, boggy region.

9. The alligator, along with snakes, lizards, and other scaly, crawling animals, is a _____.

Think about setting and mood.

10. Which words identify the setting of the reading? (Circle three.)

    the West   the South   Canada
    Louisiana   the Mississippi delta

11. In the reading, how is the *mood* of the bayou described? (Circle three.)

    hectic   mysterious   eerie
    ugly   beautiful   boring

Look it up in a reference source.

12. Write one fact about bayous that isn't mentioned in the reading.

_____
_____

READ: Do you like to play video games? Have you ever played Pac-Man?

HAPPY BIRTHDAY, PAC-MAN

In May 2005, the world's most famous video game character turned 25. But age isn't stopping little yellow Pac-Man! Copies of the original game and updated versions are still selling around the world.

Early in the history of video games, game creator Toru Iwatani was looking for a fresh idea. He wanted something that looked like a cartoon. He hoped it would appeal to adults as well as to young people. As the story goes, a brainstorm struck Iwatani at dinner. After taking a first slice of pizza, he studied the pie. It looked like a head with a big, open mouth! Iwatani pictured it racing through a maze, eating things. Then, of course, video technology wasn't what it is today. Iwatani couldn't make a character as detailed as a pizza. So Pac-Man became a yellow circle with a wedge of a mouth. His name came from the Japanese word *pakupaku*. That means "to flap one's mouth open and closed."

The game is simple to learn. It takes only a four-position joystick to guide Pac-Man. He goes through a maze gobbling up dots and avoiding "ghosts." These are colorful figures that look like upside-down sacks with eyes. If a ghost touches Pac-Man, he dies, and the game is over. With each level, the ghosts speed up and play gets harder.

Pac-Man was the first video game to name its characters. Besides the hero, there are the ghosts: Blinky, Pinky, Inky, and Clyde. With its familiar characters and catchy music, Pac-Man quickly became the hottest arcade game in history. The yellow fellow soon showed up on T-shirts, coffee mugs, cereals, and board games. In 1982, a Ms. Pac-Man game came out. The lovely lady looks like Pac-Man, but she also sports lipstick, a red bow, and a beauty mark.

Recordkeepers believe that the Pac-Man game was played more the 10 billion times in the 20th century.

REFLECT: Think about video games.

1. Do you play video games? If so, which one is your favorite? What do you like about it?

_____
_____
_____
_____

LESSON 14: HAPPY BIRTHDAY, PAC MAN

2. Have you ever played Pac-Man? Do you like the game? Tell why or why not.
   _____
   _____

3. Compare one of the new games with Pac-Man. Think about subject matter, graphics, difficulty, and about the audiences they appeal to.
   _____
   _____
   _____

RESPOND: *Circle a letter or word, fill in the blanks, or write out the answer.*

Recall details.

1. In 2005, how many years old was the Pac-Man game?
   a. 100   b. 5   c. 25

2. What sparked the idea for Pac-Man?
   a. a scary movie
   b. a partly eaten pizza
   c. a fat, yellow cat

3. The name Pac-Man comes from what language?
   a. French   b. Greek   c. Japanese

4. Who is Clyde?
   a. a ghost in the game
   b. the inventor of Pac-Man
   c. a champion Pac-Man player

5. How was Pac-Man different from earlier games?
   a. It was harder.
   b. It was more violent.
   c. Its characters had names.

6. The Pac-Man game was meant to appeal to whom?
   a. young men
   b. children
   c. all adults and young people

7. What can "kill" Pac-Man?
   a. ghosts   b. dots   c. Ms. Pac-Man

Build your vocabulary.

8. Toru Iwatani had a *brainstorm*, or a (headache / sudden brilliant idea).

9. Shaped like a *wedge*, Pac-Man's mouth is (triangular / square).

10. Moving along a (straight roadway / series of winding paths), Pac-Man gobbles his way through a *maze*.

Draw conclusions.

11. Give two reasons you think the game of Pac-Man became so popular.
    • _____
    • _____

Look it up in a reference source.

12. *Pong* and *Space Invaders* were among the earliest video games. Describe one of these games.
    _____
    _____
    _____
    _____
    _____

READ • REFLECT • RESPOND
LESSON 15

READ: *This girl has what it takes to succeed!*

RACHAEL SCDORIS: _____

Suppose a blind person wants to become a sled dog racer. Is that a realistic goal or just a fantasy? Young Rachael Scdoris of Oregon decided that her chances were good. Even though she's been legally blind since birth, she knew she could be a champ.

Rachael grew up around sled dogs and mushers (sled dog drivers). At age 11, she began racing. Throughout her teens, she trained and cared for dog teams. At 15, she became the youngest athlete to complete a 500-mile course. Rachael didn't think of herself as a "handicapped" athlete. She competed against and beat some of the top racers.

At 20, Rachael took on her biggest challenge. She entered the 2005 Iditarod, which is billed as the world's "Last Great Race." The challenging 1,200-mile race course runs from Anchorage to Nome, Alaska.

After a long debate, the Iditarod committee allowed Rachael to compete. She was permitted to carry a two-way radio and talk to another musher. He would run a team ahead of hers. He'd warn of hazards like hanging branches, broken ice, and moose on the trail. In addition to the hazard of ice on the trail, these were dangers her very limited vision might miss.

Rachael's Iditarod adventure gained world attention. Her team raced through the early checkpoints. About three-fourths of the way to the finish line, Rachael dropped out of the race. But it wasn't because of her visual challenges. She "scratched" the race because some of her dogs were ill. For Rachael, her team's well-being always comes first!

Rachael's 2005 Iditarod run inspired people. It gave them courage to meet their own challenges. The Women's Sports Foundation named her one of America's top women athletes. Today, Rachael Scdoris operates sled dog tours in Oregon. And at the same time, she's training and planning for the next Iditarod.

REFLECT: *Think about Rachael Scdoris and others who overcome a physical challenge.*

1. Which of the following do you think would make a good subtitle for this reading?

   a. Winning Is Everything!

   b. Anything Is Possible!

   c. A Dog Is a Musher's Best Friend!

2. Write two qualities a physically challenged athlete must have.

   • _____
   • _____

Lesson 15: RACHAEL SCDORIS

3. Name another sport in which human and animal athletes compete as a team. _____

RESPOND: Circle a letter or word, fill in the blanks, or write out the answer.

Put events in order.

1. The following sentences are details from the reading. Number them in chronological order.

    ____ a. Rachael Scdoris is allowed to race in the 2005 Iditarod.

    ____ b. Rachael becomes the youngest musher to complete a 500-mile course.

    ____ c. Rachael Scdoris competes in her first dog-sled race.

    ____ d. Rachael trains for the 2005 Iditarod.

Recall details.

2. Rachael Scdoris is (hard of hearing / legally blind).

3. Rachael makes her home in (Alaska / Oregon).

4. The Iditarod is a sled dog race in (Alaska / Oregon).

5. During her Iditarod run, Rachael had help (spotting hazards along the trail / taking care of her sick dogs).

6. Rachael was honored as one of America's top (blind athletes / women athletes).

7. Rachael plans to (retire from sled dog racing / enter the next Iditarod).

Build your vocabulary.

| debate   checkpoint   musher   scratch   inspire |

8. A sled dog driver is also called a _____.

9. A _____ is a discussion of the different sides of an issue.

10. A _____ is a place to stop and check in along a route.

11. To _____ from a race means to withdraw from it.

12. Something that encourages people to take action is said to _____ them.

Make a judgment.

13. Rachael's success as a dog sled racer is especially remarkable because she is: (Circle two.)

    a musher   from Oregon   young
    a pet owner   legally blind   tour guide

Look it up on the Internet.

14. Find websites that feature interviews with Rachael Scdoris. Write something interesting Rachael said in an interview.

    _____
    _____
    _____
    _____

READ•REFLECT•RESPOND

READ · REFLECT · RESPOND
LESSON 16

READ: *Why does the moon change color? Read on to find out.*

PUMPKIN MOON

The full moon is its usual pale, white color. Then something curious happens. The moon turns a brilliant red-orange! Like a giant pumpkin, it glows fat and round. This is a total eclipse of the moon.

A lunar eclipse happens when the moon passes through Earth's shadow. During a partial eclipse, only the edge of the shadow hides the moon. During a total eclipse, the entire moon hides behind the darkest part of the shadow.

A lunar eclipse occurs only when the moon is full. Although the moon orbits Earth every 29.5 days, it doesn't pass through Earth's shadow every time it goes around. That's why total lunar eclipses are somewhat rare. In one year, there may be several. In 1982, for example, there were three. In other years—such as 2005—there may be none. In 2004, a

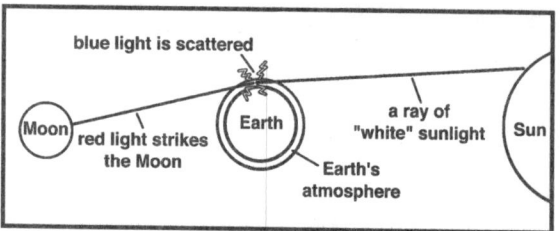

Pumpkin Moon appeared just in time for the Halloween season.

Why does the moon take on a colorful glow in a total eclipse? Because the Earth's atmosphere bends sunlight, and the rays go into the shadow.

Pure white sunlight is actually made up of many colors. Particles and gases in the Earth's atmosphere filter out and scatter the blue in the light. The remaining light is deep red or orange. The Pumpkin Moon is created when the moon reflects the red-orange light back toward Earth.

REFLECT: *Think about the moon in the night sky.*

1. Circle three words that describe a lunar eclipse.

    dangerous

    white

    red-orange

    nighttime

    daytime

    round

    crescent-shaped

2. a. Have you ever seen an eclipse of the moon or sun? _____
   b. If you answered *yes*, describe the experience. _____
   _____
   _____

3. The next total eclipse of the moon should be visible from North America on March 3, 2007. How old will you be then? Where do you think you might be living? Would you like to view the eclipse? Why or why not?
   _____
   _____
   _____

LESSON 16: PUMPKIN MOON

RESPOND: *Circle a letter or word, fill in the blanks, or write out the answer.*

Recognize a main idea.

1. Why is an eclipsed moon sometimes called a *Pumpkin Moon*?

   _____
   _____
   _____

Recall details.

2. When did North America see its last total eclipse of the moon?
   a. 1923   b. 2004   c. never

3. What causes a lunar eclipse?
   a. Earth's shadow hides the moon.
   b. The planet Mars hides the moon.
   c. The moon hides Earth.

Use the illustration in the reading to help you answer these questions.

4. What color is pure sunlight?
   a. blue   b. red   c. white

5. What happens when a ray of sunlight hits Earth's atmosphere?
   a. The light bounces back to the sun.
   b. All light is blocked.
   c. Blue light is filtered out.

6. What color is the light that continues on to the moon?
   a. blue   b. red   c. white

7. What does the illustration explain?
   a. the difference between a solar and lunar eclipse
   b. why a lunar eclipse creates a red-orange Pumpkin Moon
   c. why there are full moons, half moons, and crescent moons

Build your vocabulary.

8. A total *lunar eclipse* occurred in 2004.
   • The word *lunar* means "having to do with (Earth / the moon)."
   • An *eclipse* is the (exploration of / darkening and hiding of) the sun or the moon.

9. During an eclipse, the moon passes through Earth's *shadow*.
   • A *shadow* is (the light given off by a heavenly body / the dark shape cast by something as it cuts off light).

10. Earth's *atmosphere* bends light rays.
    • The word *atmosphere* means the (air and gases around a planet / stars in the sky).

11. The moon *orbits* Earth.
    • To *orbit* something is to (shine light on / circle around) it.

12. In a *partial* eclipse, only the edge of the shadow hides the moon.
    • The word *partial* means (not complete / complete).

Look it up in a reference source.

13. Write one fact about the *moon* or a *lunar eclipse* that is not included in the reading.

    _____
    _____
    _____
    _____

READ · REFLECT · RESPOND
LESSON 17

READ: *How much change can one courageous man bring about?*

CESAR CHAVEZ FIGHTS FOR *LA CAUSA*

"*Viva la causa!* Long live the cause!" That was the cry of Cesar Chavez and the United Farm Workers. It was 1965, and California's Mexican-American farm workers were calling for change. They wanted fair wages and decent working conditions. If they had to, they would strike.

Cesar Chavez had begun life 38 years earlier on his family's small farm in Arizona. When he was 10, the Great Depression struck and his family lost their farm. Along with thousands of others, they headed for California. There they worked the fields. As migrant workers, they moved often, following farming seasons. Sometimes the Chavez family lived in shacks. Sometimes they slept in their car. As they labored long, hot hours for little pay, Cesar dreamed of a better life.

Cesar attended about 36 different grammar schools. He quit school after grade eight, but he never quit learning. Most importantly, he learned to make his voice heard.

Cesar Chavez decided that farm workers had to help themselves. In 1962, he formed a union. In 1965, he convinced workers to overcome their fears. They launched a strike against grape growers. At first, *La Causa*, "The Cause," seemed hopeless. But the farm workers were fighting for their children's future. People saw justice in their struggle. Many college students and community leaders supported *La Causa*. By 1968, Chavez was leading a national boycott of California table grapes.

Chavez insisted that the strike be nonviolent. Even *La Causa*, he said, was not worth a single life. To show his resolve, he fasted. For 25 days Chavez ate nothing and drank only water. His determination encouraged others. In 1970, both grape growers and union workers signed a contract.

The famous labor leader died in 1993. In 1994, President Clinton presented the U.S. Medal of Freedom in Chavez's name. He'd shown how to effectively fight injustice—without violence.

REFLECT: *Think about Cesar Chavez and his fight for farm workers' rights.*

1. Circle one word in each pair that describes Cesar Chavez.

   violent / nonviolent   determined / weak   leader / follower   selfish / unselfish

2. Circle two things that workers do when they go on strike.

   stay home from their jobs   work harder at their jobs
   advertise for their employer   carry signs to raise public awareness

3. What are some reasons why workers might strike? Why might a strike force an employer to make changes?

   _____
   _____

4. Imagine you could improve the lives of workers if you stopped buying your favorite food. Would you be willing to do it? Explain your answer.

   _____
   _____

RESPOND: Circle a letter or word, fill in the blanks, or write out the answer.

Recall details.

1. What was the United Farm Workers?
   a. a group of California grape growers
   b. a union created by Cesar Chavez

2. What is the meaning of *La Causa*?
   a. The Cause   b. The Dream

3. Where was the struggle described in the reading?
   a. Mexico   b. California

4. What two things did the farm workers do to bring about change?
   a. burned fields and smashed grapes
   b. went on strike and started a boycott

5. How did Chavez show his dedication and inspire his fellow workers?
   a. He shaved his head.
   b. He went without food.

Build your vocabulary.

6. A group of people joined together for a purpose is a u ___ ___ ___ n.

7. The Gr ___ ___ ___ D ___ pr ___ ___ ___ ___ ___ ___ n was a period in American history.

8. A m ___ ___ ___ ___ ___ ___ t worker is a farm laborer who moves from place to place to pick seasonal crops.

9. To b ___ ___ ___ ___ ___ ___ ___ something is to stop buying, selling, or using it.

10. Chavez believed in n ___ nv ___ ___ ___ ___ ___ ___ ___ protest. He would not use physical force to get what he wanted.

11. To give his followers courage, Chavez f ___ s ___ ___ ___, or went without food.

Look it up in a reference source.

12. When was Cesar Chavez born? When did he die? Write the month, day, and year.

    BORN: _____

    DIED: _____

READ · REFLECT · RESPOND

LESSON 18

READ: *Do you know these basic facts about blood?*

BLOOD: THE LIFESTREAM OF YOUR BODY

Blood makes up 7–8 percent of your body weight. It carries oxygen and food to all your body parts through a vast network of blood vessels. And blood does more than just carry food and oxygen. It fights disease germs and also helps the body to get rid of wastes.

The amount of blood in a body depends on the person's size. A 160-pound adult has about five quarts of blood. An 80-pound child has only about 2½ quarts. The volume of blood in a healthy person remains nearly the same at all times. This stability is important. A sharp decrease in volume from uncontrolled bleeding could result in death.

Many organs of the body collaborate to keep the blood functioning. The heart pumps the blood through the body. The lungs supply it with oxygen, and the kidneys keep it pure and free of poisons. Other organs help, too. The liver and the intestines, for example, supply blood with food and keep it in healthy working order.

Human blood can be divided into four main groups or types—A, B, AB, and O. In the United States, about 45 percent of the population has type O blood. About 41 percent has type A blood, and some 10 percent has type B blood. Only four percent has type AB blood.

Before performing a blood transfusion, doctors are very careful to match the donor's blood type with the patient's. Otherwise, the patient could suffer a dangerous reaction. Combining certain blood groups causes substances in the blood to "clump," or stick together. And clumping can block small blood vessels and cause serious illness or even death.

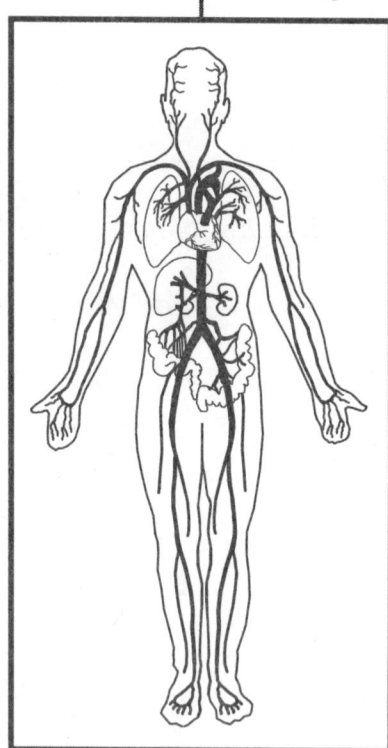

LAID END TO END, THE BLOOD VESSELS IN THE HUMAN BODY WOULD TOTAL 100,000 MILES IN LENGTH.

REFLECT: *Think about your inner body.*

1. Circle the words that could be used to describe blood.

    solid   vital   synthetic   liquid

    red   toxic   transparent   gritty

2. Circle the words that name *organs* of the human body.

    skin   blood   hair   stomach

    toenails   knuckles   heart   teeth

LESSON 18: BLOOD: THE LIFESTREAM OF YOUR BODY

RESPOND: Circle a letter or word, fill in the blanks, or write out the answer.

Recall details. (Write T for true or F for false.)

1. ____ Blood keeps the kidneys free of poisons.

2. ____ Most people in the United States have either type O or type A blood.

3. ____ Uncontrolled bleeding increases blood volume.

4. ____ Blood helps the body resist diseast.

Build your vocabulary. (Complete words from the reading.)

5. To c_ _ _ _ _ _ _ _ _ _ is to work together to accomplish something.

6. A system of interconnected lines or other things is called a n_ _ _ _ _ _ _.

7. V_ _ _ _ _ _ are tubes in the body through which a fluid flows.

8. A t_ _ _ _ _ _ _ _ _ _ _ is the transfer of blood from a healthy donor to someone else's bloodstream.

Match synonyms.

| transports | provides | attacks | depends |

9. relies / _____

10. supply / _____

11. fights / _____

12. carries / _____

Activate prior knowledge.

13. The major blood vessels in the body are called
    a. ligaments and tendons.
    b. arteries and veins.
    c. platelets and plasma.

Draw conclusions.

14. A nurse at a blood bank draws one pint of blood from each donor. How many donors would it take to collect three quarts of blood?
    a. 12   b. 6   c. 8

15. What percent of people in the United States do *not* have type AB blood?
    a. 94%   b. 51%   c. 96%

16. Severe disease in what organ could limit the blood's supply of oxygen?
    a. lungs
    b. stomach
    c. intestines

Look it up in a reference source.

17. *Anemia* is a blood condition that causes people to become pale and weak. Describe this condition and explain its cause.

    _____
    _____
    _____
    _____
    _____
    _____

READ•REFLECT•RESPOND 41

READ · REFLECT · RESPOND
LESSON 19

READ: *Could you live the life of a samurai warrior?*

SAMURAI WARRIORS

Stretch your imagination back some 800 years to the island nation of Japan. You've landed in a time when an emperor ruled from the imperial capital. Although he lived in splendor, the emperor was only the formal ruler. The real power was held by a military leader, or shogun. The shogun granted lands to local warlords. Each warlord protected his region with an army of highly trained warriors. These armies battled for power.

The warriors were called *samurai* (SAM oo rye). That word means "those who serve." The samurai could be compared to the knights of Europe. Like knights, they had high social status. They were also heavily armed and well-trained for war. On the battlefield, they wore elaborate suits of armor.

The samurai lived by a code of honor known as *bushido* (BOO shee doh). Meaning "the way of the warrior," bushido demanded fierce loyalty to the warlord. It called for honor and bravery. Most importantly, a warrior must not fear death. In fact, a samurai who dishonored himself was expected to end his own life. Each samurai carried both a long sword and a short one. If necessary, he would use the short sword to end his own life. The samurai could also fight without weapons. He was highly trained in martial arts.

Japanese society greatly respected the samurai. This was more than just a job. It was a social class as well. The warriors and their families lived in fine houses near the warlord's castle.

The position of samurai was often inherited. A boy would be "born" a samurai because his father had been one. Only samurai could carry swords. If a boy played with a wooden sword, everyone knew he was a samurai. A young samurai learned to do more than make war. He learned to read and write, and he studied literature. To learn to tolerate pain, he walked barefoot in snow. All day every day he followed strict rules. Living as a samurai was not easy!

REFLECT: *Think about samurai warriors and ancient Japan.*

1. Circle words that could describe a samurai.

uneducated	well-educated	loyal	fearful	follower	warrior
admired	looked down upon	proud	ashamed	brave	pacifist

2. Name two things about being a samurai that you think would be good.

   - _____
   - _____

3. Name two things about being a samurai that you think would be bad.

   - _____
   - _____

RESPOND: *Circle a letter or word, fill in the blanks, or write out the answer.*

Match word and meaning.

1. ____ emperor
2. ____ warlord
3. ____ shogun
4. ____ samurai

   a. the powerful head of a region of ancient Japan
   b. person who rules an entire group of countries
   c. member of the warrior class of ancient Japan
   d. local ruler who controls a military force

Recall details.

5. What is the meaning of the word *samurai*?
   _____

6. What is the meaning of the word *bushido*?
   _____

7. Circle three requirements of *bushido*.

   | honor | wealth | bravery |
   | beauty | loyalty | gentleness |

8. Who had the real power of government in ancient Japan?
   a. the samurai
   b. the emperor
   c. the shogun

9. What was the main job of the samurai?
   a. to guard the emperor
   b. to fight for their local warlord
   c. to become a scholar

10. Which would cause a samurai to take his own life?
    a. killing another human being
    b. displaying fear in battle
    c. reading a book

11. Where did the samurai families live?
    a. in tents on the battlefield
    b. in the village with the peasants
    c. in homes near the castle

Make a comparison.

12. Explain two ways that samurai warriors were like European knights.
    - _____
      _____
    - _____
      _____

Look it up in a reference source.

13. Japanese *karate* is still a popular martial art. Learn something about karate. Write one or two facts below.
    _____
    _____
    _____

READ · REFLECT · RESPOND
LESSON 20

READ: *Take a deep breath and read on.*

HOW ANIMALS BREATHE

What do all animals—including humans—have in common? One trait we share is our need for oxygen. We can't live without it! All animals have body parts that do the job of bringing in oxygen.

Human beings belong to the animal class called *mammals*. Mammals are warmblooded and have a backbone. Female mammals have glands that produce milk for feeding their young. Mammals breathe air into their bodies through their noses. Special organs, the *lungs*, take in oxygen from that air.

Insects, who are members of another class of animal, have no lungs. They breathe through small holes called *spiracles*. These openings are in the sides of their bodies. Spiracles lead into branching air tubes. These tubes take oxygen from the air and carry it to the bloodstream.

Fish live underwater. They do not get oxygen through the air. In fact, if they are out of water for too long, they will die from a lack of oxygen. Gills are the breathing organs of fish and many other water-dwelling animals. As water flows into a fish's body, it passes through its gills. The gills contain blood vessels that carry oxygen from the water throughout the body.

What about whales? Because they're fish-shaped swimmers, people often think they breathe through gills. But whales, in fact, are not fish. Just like other mammals, a whale will drown if it's underwater too long. When a whale is underwater, it closes its nostrils and holds its breath!

MAMMALS 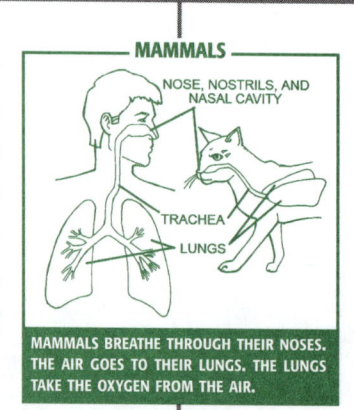
MAMMALS BREATHE THROUGH THEIR NOSES. THE AIR GOES TO THEIR LUNGS. THE LUNGS TAKE THE OXYGEN FROM THE AIR.

FISH 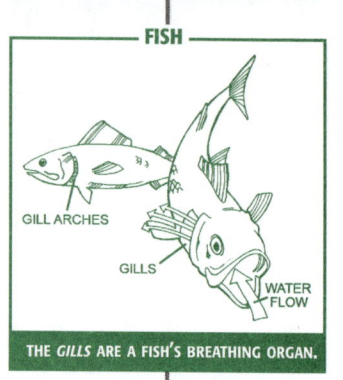
THE *GILLS* ARE A FISH'S BREATHING ORGAN.

INSECTS 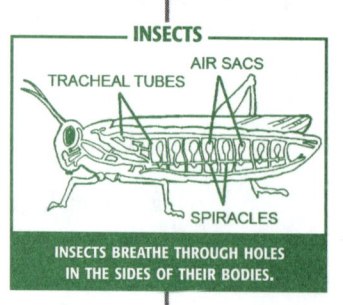
INSECTS BREATHE THROUGH HOLES IN THE SIDES OF THEIR BODIES.

REFLECT: *Think about how animals breathe.*

1. Human beings take in air through their noses. What other job does a nose do?

    _____

2. Name another animal that breathes the way human beings do.

    _____

3. Name another animal that breathes the way a grasshopper does.

    _____

4. Circle four animals that are *fish*.

    trout   seal   salmon
    carp   guppy   sea otter

LESSON 20: HOW ANIMALS BREATHE

RESPOND: Circle a letter or word, fill in the blanks, or write out the answer.

Recall details.

1. All mammals are _____ blooded.

2. In mammals, the _____ take oxygen from the air.

3. Insects breathe through small holes called _____.

4. Fish have breathing organs called _____.

Recognize a main idea.

5. According to the reading, all animals need
   a. love.
   b. air.
   c. oxygen.

Use the diagrams in the reading.

6. A human being takes air into the body through its
   a. lungs.
   b. nose.
   c. blood vessels.

7. Gills help water animals
   a. protect their young.
   b. get oxygen from air.
   c. get oxygen from water.

8. Three different classes of animals are
   a. human beings, cows, and whales.
   b. mammals, insects, and fish.
   c. lungs, gills, and spiracles.

Build your vocabulary.

9. O _ _ _ _ _ is a colorless, odorless gas that animals need to stay alive.

10. A b _ _ _ _ v _ _ _ _ _ _ is one of the body's many tubes through which blood flows.

11. Like the heart, a part of the body that has a special purpose is an o _ _ _ _ _.

12. To take air in and let it out is to b _ _ _ _ _ _.

13. A puff of air taken in or let out is a b _ _ _ _ _.

Look it up in a reference source.

14. How does each of the following animals get oxygen?

    An eel: _____

    A dolphin: _____

    A bird: _____

    A bee: _____

    A pig: _____

READ•REFLECT•RESPOND 45

READ • REFLECT • RESPOND
LESSON 21

READ: *What would you see if you visited Death Valley?*

TITLE: _____

Death Valley! The name suggests a gloomy, lifeless place. But it's not so! Located in east-central California, Death Valley National Park is an amazing site. It is among the world's most unusual settings and one of the most interesting.

Part of the Mohave Desert, Death Valley is a land of extremes. It is one of Earth's hottest regions. In summer average temperatures top 100 degrees Fahrenheit. The valley's lowest point is Badwater Basin. At 282 feet below sea level, Badwater is the lowest spot in the Western Hemisphere. Death Valley is also the driest place in North America. Why? Surrounding mountain ranges block rain storms. On an average, less than two inches of rain fall in a year.

Despite the harsh climate, life abounds in the valley. More than 1,000 kinds of plants grow there. They've adapted to the arid land. Seeking moisture, some send their roots deep. Others store water in leaves and stems.

In spring, a little rain falls. Then colorful wildflowers carpet the valley. Higher areas have more moisture. Juniper trees and pines live on slopes that rise from the valley floor. In winter, snow blankets surrounding peaks.

Some animals, like lizards, thrive in Death Valley's heat. But other desert dwellers, like coyotes, foxes, and bobcats, only come forth when the hot sun goes down.

Few large animals live in the park. Small herds of bighorn sheep roam the higher, cooler slopes. Herds of wild burros have lived in Death Valley. They were offspring of pack animals used in the California Gold Rush. The greedy burros left little food for native wildlife. So most of them have been removed from the park.

With searing heat and record-breaking dryness, Death Valley earns a visitor's respect. All who spend time there are likely to say, "There's nothing else like this on Earth!"

REFLECT: *Think about Death Valley, California, and desert life.*

1. Circle three adjectives that describe Death Valley.

humid	rain-soaked	dry
unusual	lifeless	mild
hot	gloomy	icy

2. Circle four items a visitor to Death Valley would most likely need.

umbrella	raincoat	canteen
tuxedo	sunscreen	swim fins
sunglasses	galoshes	visored hat

LESSON 21: (to be titled by student)

3. What's the hottest place you've ever been? How hot was it?
   _____
   _____
   _____

4. Which title best fits this article? Circle the letter. Write the title above the article.
   a. The History of Death Valley
   b. Deserts of the World
   c. The Unusual World of Death Valley

RESPOND: Circle a letter or word, fill in the blanks, or write out the answer.

Make comparisons.

1. When it comes to temperatures, Death Valley is one of the world's *h*_____ places.

2. Badwater Basin is the *l*_____ point in the *W*_____ *H*_____.

3. Having so little rainfall, Death Valley is the *d*_____ place in *n*_____ *a*_____.

Recall details.

4. Name two features that allow some Death Valley plants to live with little water.
   • _____
   • _____

5. Name two kinds of trees found on slopes around Death Valley.
   • _____
   • _____

6. What animal was brought in by gold miners?
   • _____

7. List three animals living in Death Valley.
   • _____
   • _____
   • _____

Use the map in the reading.

8. Death Valley is in (eastern / western) California.

9. Death Valley is on the (Pacific Ocean / Nevada border).

10. Las Vegas is (east / west) of Death Valley.

11. Los Angeles is (east / west) of Death Valley.

Build your vocabulary.

12. A *gloomy* places gives off a (steamy / sad) feeling.

13. A (*herd* / *colony*) is a number of large animals living together.

14. Healthy animals and plants that grow well are said to (*survive* / *thrive*).

Look it up in a reference source.

15. Write a fact about Death Valley that is not mentioned in the reading.
    _____
    _____

READ•REFLECT•RESPOND 47

Read · Reflect · Respond
Lesson 22

Read: *Don't have your own wheels? Not a problem!*

HOW TO RIDE A BUS . . . AND MORE!

How do you ride the bus? That's easy! You get on, pay your fare, and sit down. What's the big deal?

Actually, taking full advantage of a city bus system *is* a big deal! Lots of information is available to help you make the most of your public transit system. Where can you find it?

Most city bus systems have a web site. You can look online for bus routes and schedules, as well as for fare information. Automatic "trip planners" allow users to type in their starting point, destination, and preferred time schedule. Then the service helps them plan their itineraries. It suggests the best bus line, bus stops, and departure and arrival times. If you don't have access to a computer, a phone number is usually listed. A local phone book may also list some information. Most libraries, post offices, banks, and shopping centers provide free bus schedules and route maps.

City transit is accessible to almost everyone. Reduced fares are usually offered to seniors and riders with disabilities. Ramps and lifts provide access to wheelchair passengers and others who can't climb steps. There's usually a special easy-seating area near the front of the bus. Service animals, such as seeing-eye dogs, are usually welcome. Bus schedules are also available in large print or on audio cassette for riders who need them.

GROVE CITY RAPID TRANSIT

ROUTE 63: WEEKDAY SCHEDULE TO GROVE CITY PARK

TOWN CENTER SQUARE	3RD & FISHER	8TH & LAKE	15TH & CLARK	GROVE CITY PARK
14, 22, 32, 78, 80		*19*		*16, 28, 37, 50*
6:48 A.M.	6:53 A.M.	7:00 A.M.	7:12 A.M.	7:30 A.M.
7:30 A.M.	7:35 A.M.	7:42 A.M.	7:54 A.M.	8:12 A.M.
9:15 A.M.	9:20 A.M.	9:27 A.M.	9:39 A.M.	9:57 A.M.
10:25 A.M.	10:30 A.M.	10:37 A.M.	10:49 A.M.	11:01 A.M.

HOW TO READ BUS SCHEDULE:
- Reading from top to bottom tells you the departure time at each scheduled stop.
- To figure out how long it takes to get from point to point along the route, read the times from left to right.
- Numbers listed in italics under the stop points show transfer lines.

Reflect: *Think about your local bus system.*

1. What's the name of your local transit company? _____

2. Other than buses, are there more public transit options in your city or town? What are they? (Examples would be rail lines, subways, trams, or streetcars.)

_____

LESSON 22: HOW TO RIDE A BUS . . . AND MORE!

3. What are some of the benefits and disadvantages of traveling by bus?
   _____
   _____

4. Think about your city or town. List three popular destination points that might appear on a bus route map.
   • _____   • _____   • _____

RESPOND: Circle a letter or word, fill in the blanks, or write out the answer.

Identify main ideas.

1. What's the main idea of the reading?
   a. Reading a bus schedule is easy.
   b. City bus systems have a lot to offer everyone.

2. What's the main purpose of a bus schedule?
   a. to trace the route of a certain bus line
   b. to tell what time a bus reaches each stop along the route

Recall details.

3. Circle three items of information you can find on a bus schedule.

when a bus arrives at certain stops	how long it takes to get from one stop to the next
which stops are transfer points	if the bus is running on time that day

4. Describe two ways transit companies help riders with disabilities.
   • _____
     _____
   • _____
     _____

5. List three public places a bus rider might pick up a printed schedule.
   • _____
   • _____
   • _____

6. What are two other ways a person might get a bus route schedule?
   • _____
   • _____

Build your vocabulary.

7. At a *transfer* point, a rider can (buy a weekly pass / change to a different bus route).

8. An *itinerary* is a (large city bus / trip plan).

9. A *destination* is the (place a person is going / starting point of a trip).

10. The *departure* is the time a bus (leaves / arrives).

Use the schedule.

11. It takes bus #63 _____ minutes to travel from Town Center Square to 3rd & Fisher.

12. A rider who catches bus #63 at 8th & Lake at 9:27 will get to Grove City Park at _____.

13. A rider who misses the 7:30 A.M. bus at Town Center Square will have to wait _____ minutes for the next one.

14. A rider can transfer from line #63 to line #19 at the _____ stop.

READ • REFLECT • RESPOND   49

Read · Reflect · Respond
LESSON 23

Read: *Have you ever heard someone say, "Beware of Greeks bearing gifts!"?*

THE TROJAN HORSE

This Greek myth begins with a handsome Trojan named Paris. He'd made the mistake of angering the goddesses, Hera and Athena. Luckily, however, he was in the good graces of the goddess Aphrodite. She promised him the most beautiful woman in the world.

That's when trouble began. The world's most beautiful woman was Helen of Troy. Unfortunately, she was already married to Menelaus, the king of Sparta. But Paris took Aphrodite up on her promise. He claimed Helen as his own and carried her off to Troy. To reclaim his wife, Menelaus and an army of Greek warriors sailed for Troy.

Nine years of war followed. Finally, the Greeks surrounded Troy—but they couldn't get inside its walls. The Greek soldiers had an idea. They pretended to give up and retreat to their ships. Yet all the while, they were building a huge, hollow, wooden horse.

One night, the Greeks pulled the horse to the gates of Troy. Then some of the soldiers boarded the ships and sailed away. At dawn, the Trojans rejoiced when they saw that their enemy's ships were gone. Then they saw the giant wooden horse at the gate.

"It's a peace offering!" someone exclaimed.

Others were more wary. "I don't trust our enemies," one citizen said. *"Beware of Greeks bearing gifts!"*

The Trojans should have listened to the skeptical citizen. Instead, they pulled the "gift" inside the gates. That night, as the Trojans slept, a secret door in the horse swung open. Soldiers climbed out, crept to the walls, and unlocked the gates. The Greek army poured into the city. Six hours later, Troy was in ruins!

Reflect: *Think about Greek mythology and the tale of the Trojan horse.*

1. The tale of the Trojan horse is about
   a. a famous trick.
   b. an evil king.
   c. a new invention.

2. The ancient Greeks believed that
   a. the gods had human-like personalities.
   b. there was only one true god.
   c. good people can become godlike.

3. You might say, "Beware of Greeks bearing gifts!" when
   a. your best friend gives you a birthday present.
   b. someone who dislikes you brings you a gift.
   c. a store clerk gives you a discount on a purchase.

LESSON 23: THE TROJAN HORSE

RESPOND: Circle a letter or word, fill in the blanks, or write out the answer.

Recall details.

1. Paris came from the city of _____.

2. _____ was said to be the most beautiful woman in the world.

3. Menelaus was Helen's _____.

4. The Trojan War lasted for _____ years.

5. Greek soldiers hid in a giant, wooden _____.

6. The war ended in the destruction of the city of _____.

Put details in order.

7. Number the events to show the order in which they happened.

   ___ Paris steals Helen and takes her to Troy.

   ___ The Greek soldiers leave a wooden horse at the gates of Troy.

   ___ A goddess promises Paris the most beautiful woman in the world.

   ___ Menelaus gathers an army and sails to Troy.

   ___ Soldiers climb out of the wooden horse.

Build your vocabulary.

8. "Beware of Greeks bearing gifts!" is an old *adage*.
   - Two other words for *adage* are (summary / saying / proverb).

9. An ancient Greek *myth* describes the fall of a city called Troy.
   - Two other words for *myth* are (legend / oath / story).

10. The Greek soldiers pretended to *retreat* to their ships.
    - Two other words for *retreat* are (withdraw / leave / advance).

11. The Trojans should have listened to the *skeptical* citizen.
    - Two other words for *skeptical* are (suspicious / gullible / doubting).

Draw a conclusion.

12. "Beware of Greeks bearing gifts!" warns you to _____
    _____
    _____
    _____
    _____

Look it up in a reference source.

13. Write a fact about ancient Troy that is not mentioned in the reading.
    _____
    _____
    _____
    _____

READ · REFLECT · RESPOND
LESSON 24

READ: *Give a chimp a paintbrush, and who knows what might happen?*

CHIMP ART

In the 1950s, animal expert Desmond Morris encouraged a chimpanzee named Congo to paint. Morris wanted to know if a chimp could "create order through art." By the time Congo was two, he'd stopped eating the brushes and actually begun to paint!

Congo's works could be described as "modern" or "abstract" art. Some critics say they're nothing more than scribbles. Others compliment his "bold strokes." Clearly, Congo has had admirers—including Pablo Picasso! The great artist is said to have framed and hung a "Congo original" in his own studio!

In 2005, three of Congo's artworks were offered for sale at a London art auction. Congo's paintings appeared alongside those of some famous human artists! The sale's art director said he included the chimp's paintings as a lark. He described Congo's work as "brightly colored with bold brushstrokes." Together the three paintings were expected to sell for around $1,500.

Congo's art was the hit of the auction! When the bidding closed, an American had purchased the chimp's paintings for more than $25,000!

Before he died at age 10, Congo had created about 400 artworks. Considering the recent sales price, art dealers are sure to be looking for more Congo originals!

REFLECT: *Think about "modern" art and this most unusual artist.*

1. Some people think all abstract art looks like animal scratchings. What is your opinion of modern art?

   _____
   _____
   _____

2. Why might someone want to own a chimp painting?

   _____
   _____
   _____

LESSON 24: CHIMP ART

3. Do you think chimpanzees are intelligent animals? Give reasons and/or examples to support your answer.

_____
_____
_____

RESPOND: *Circle a letter or word, fill in the blanks, or write out the answer.*

Identify the main idea.

1. The reading is about
    a. the surprising interest in Congo's paintings.
    b. how to teach a chimpanzee to paint.
    c. how hard it is to understand abstract art.

Recall details.

2. To become an artist, what did Congo have to stop doing?
    a. ignoring his trainer
    b. eating paintbrushes
    c. playing board games

3. What type of art did Congo create?
    a. landscapes
    b. abstracts
    c. photographs

4. At the auction, Congo's paintings sold for
    a. less than expected.
    b. a little more than expected.
    c. much more than expected.

Build your vocabulary.

5. *Abstract* art is
    a. formed with designs, not actually like a real thing.
    b. as clearly realistic as a photograph.

6. An *auction* is a
    a. group meeting where people give opinions about things.
    b. public sale where things are sold to the highest bidder.

7. To *bid* on something is to
    a. offer a purchase price for it.
    b. advertise it in the newspaper.

Draw a conclusion.

8. The reading suggests that paintings gain value after the artist dies. Does Congo's story support that idea? Why or why not?

_____
_____
_____

9. Why might a painting become more valuable after the artist's death?

_____
_____
_____

Look it up in a reference source.

10. Check out some paintings by Pablo Picasso. Give your opinion of his work.

_____
_____
_____

READ•REFLECT•RESPOND 53

READ · REFLECT · RESPOND
LESSON 25

READ: *Do you have the right stuff? These two amazing women surely did!*

ANGELS ON EARTH: CLARA BARTON AND FLORENCE NIGHTINGALE

It takes a special person to be a good nurse. Nursing requires compassion, selflessness, and physical and emotional strength. The occupation has an honorable past. Two of history's most famous nurses are Clara Barton and Florence Nightingale. Both women lived and worked in the 19th century. Barton was born in 1821 and died in 1912. Nightingale lived from 1820 to 1910.

American Clara Barton began nursing during the Civil War. Horrified by the suffering of wounded soldiers, she volunteered to go to the front lines. Soon she was nicknamed the "Angel of the Battlefield" for the way she tended the injured. She soon became Superintendent of Union Nurses. At war's end, she organized searches for missing soldiers. Because of her work, more than 12,000 Civil War soldiers came to rest in marked graves.

Later, Barton visited Europe. There, she saw the International Red Cross providing aid to disaster victims. On her return home, she worked to create the American Red Cross. She became its first president.

Meanwhile, an English nurse was doing similar work. As a child, Florence Nightingale had begun care-giving by tending "sick" dolls. Later, she nursed ailing family members. When England went to war, she took her nursing skills to the battlefields of Turkey. The military soon made her "Lady-in-Chief" of nurses.

Florence made nightly hospital rounds. She carried a lantern from bed to bed, whispering comforting words to the wounded men. Grateful soldiers called her the "Lady with the Lamp."

With Nightingale in charge, hospital death rates dropped from 40% to 2%. Florence Nightingale became an authority on nursing methods. The United States asked her advice when Civil War hospitals were first set up.

CLARA BARTON

FLORENCE NIGHTINGALE

REFLECT: **Think about the work of nurses.**

1. List three places a nurse might work.
   - _____
   - _____
   - _____

2. Why would someone choose to become a nurse? List three reasons.
   - _____
   - _____
   - _____

LESSON 25: ANGELS ON EARTH: CLARA BARTON AND FLORENCE NIGHTINGALE

3. What would a nurse today have in common with the two women described in the reading?
   _____
   _____

4. Tell about a time a nurse helped you or someone you know.
   _____
   _____

RESPOND: *Circle a letter or word, fill in the blanks, or write out the answer.*

Make comparisons.

1. Name two things that Clara Barton and Florence Nightingale had in common.
   - _____
   - _____

2. Name one difference between the two women.
   _____

Recognize sequence.

3. Number these events to show the order in which they happened.

   ____ Barton began a search for missing Civil War soldiers.

   ____ Barton volunteered to be a battlefield nurse.

   ____ Barton became the first president of the American Red Cross.

4. Number these events to show the order in which they happened.

   ____ Nightingale carried a lamp on nighttime hospital rounds.

   ____ Nightingale became a military nurse.

   ____ Nightingale cared for sick cousins and aunts.

Build your vocabulary.

5. A nurse is unusually *selfless*. *Selfless* means
   a. self-confident, sure of oneself.
   b. unselfish, giving of oneself.

6. Nursing has an *honorable* past. *Honorable* means
   a. worthy of admiration and praise.
   b. difficult and full of problems.

7. Florence Nightingale nursed *ailing* family members. *Ailing* means
   a. old.   b. sick.

8. Florence became a *legend*. A *legend* is a person who
   a. does a good job.
   b. is well-known for being remarkable.

9. Nightingale was an *authority* on nursing. An *authority* is
   a. an expert.   b. a skilled soldier.

Draw a conclusion.

10. Why would Barton and Nightingale be described as "angels on earth"?
    a. because they died in battle.
    b. because they generously helped others.

READ•REFLECT•RESPOND 55

READ · REFLECT · RESPOND
LESSON 26

READ: *Use pyramid power to eat healthy!*

A NUTRITION UPDATE

There's a new model for healthful eating. In 2005, the United States Department of Agriculture (USDA) revised its old Food Pyramid. The new chart shown below reflects the latest research about a balanced diet. What's the latest plan? How does it differ from the old one?

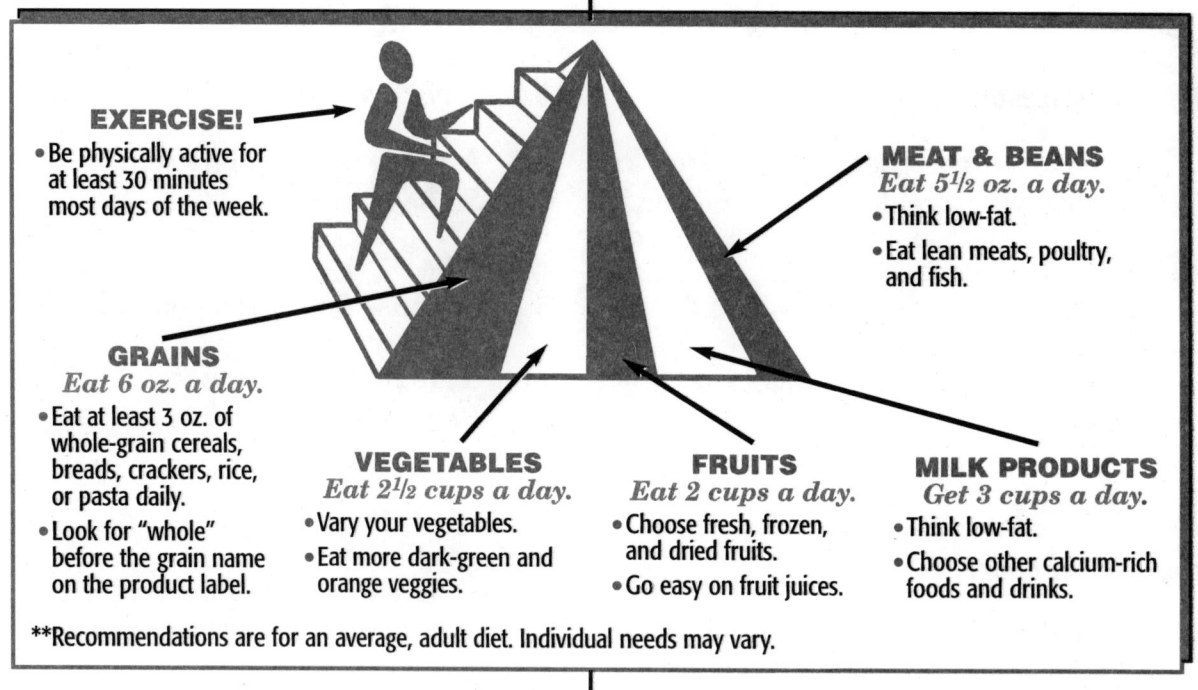

EXERCISE!
- Be physically active for at least 30 minutes most days of the week.

GRAINS
Eat 6 oz. a day.
- Eat at least 3 oz. of whole-grain cereals, breads, crackers, rice, or pasta daily.
- Look for "whole" before the grain name on the product label.

VEGETABLES
Eat 2½ cups a day.
- Vary your vegetables.
- Eat more dark-green and orange veggies.

FRUITS
Eat 2 cups a day.
- Choose fresh, frozen, and dried fruits.
- Go easy on fruit juices.

MEAT & BEANS
Eat 5½ oz. a day.
- Think low-fat.
- Eat lean meats, poultry, and fish.

MILK PRODUCTS
Get 3 cups a day.
- Think low-fat.
- Choose other calcium-rich foods and drinks.

**Recommendations are for an average, adult diet. Individual needs may vary.

Did you notice that foods at the left make up the largest part of the daily diet? In other words, for healthful eating, choose more foods from the left and fewer from the right. It's important, though, to include *some* foods from each group.

There are differences between the old and new pyramids. As its smallest food group, the old pyramid included "FATS, OILS, and SWEETS." The 2005 pyramid does not label this category as one of its food groups. The old pyramid also described healthful eating in terms of "servings" per day. Since ideas about serving size differ, the new pyramid is more specific. It describes portions in terms of cups and ounces (oz.).

REFLECT: *Think about the new food pyramid and your own diet.*

1. Compare the USDA's suggestions with your own diet. First, fill in the recommended amount. Then compare your own intake.

   GRAINS:

   DAILY RECOMMENDATION: _____   **ABOUT HOW MUCH DO YOU EAT IN A DAY?** _____

LESSON 26: A NUTRITION UPDATE

VEGETABLES:
DAILY RECOMMENDATION: _____ ABOUT HOW MUCH DO YOU EAT IN A DAY? _____

FRUITS:
DAILY RECOMMENDATION: _____ ABOUT HOW MUCH DO YOU EAT IN A DAY? _____

MILK PRODUCTS:
DAILY RECOMMENDATION: _____ ABOUT HOW MUCH DO YOU EAT IN A DAY? _____

MEAT & BEANS:
DAILY RECOMMENDATION: _____ ABOUT HOW MUCH DO YOU EAT IN A DAY? _____

2. If you wanted to eat more healthfully, what one dietary change would you make?
   _____

Respond: *Circle a letter or word, fill in the blanks, or write out the answer.*

Recall details.

1. The Pyramid shows the largest part of a good daily diet coming from which group?
   a. grains
   b. fruits
   c. meat and beans

2. The Pyramid recommends that the smallest portion come from which group?
   a. vegetables
   b. milk products
   c. meat and beans

3. The Pyramid advises people to do what?
   a. Eat every two hours
   b. Think low-fat!
   c. Use the old pyramid.

4. Which is NOT mentioned on the Food Pyramid?
   a. chocolate
   b. dried fruit
   c. cereal

Make a comparison.

5. What are two differences between the old Food Pyramid and the new one?
   • _____
   _____
   • _____
   _____

Draw a conclusion.

6. Would it be more healthful to eat light-green iceberg lettuce or dark-green spinach?
   _____

7. Would it be more healthful to drink a lot of apple juice or eat fresh apples?
   _____

8. Would it be better to drink cream, whole milk, or low-fat milk?
   _____

9. Which would be a healthier choice—white bread or whole wheat bread?
   _____

10. A person who doesn't eat red meat could get needed protein from what other sources?
    _____

READ•REFLECT•RESPOND

Read · Reflect · Respond
LESSON 27

Read: *Given the right circumstances, would you take up arms?*

WORDS FROM HISTORY: *GIVE ME LIBERTY . . .*

It was March 23, 1775. Colonial patriots had gathered in Saint John's Church in Richmond, Virginia. This group, the lawmakers of the Virginia colony, were called the House of Burgesses. They were holding an important debate that day. Should the colonists take military action against the British? Should they go to war?

A politician stood. The room fell silent. This man, Patrick Henry, was already known as a brilliant speaker. Trained as an attorney, he would one day be called "the greatest orator who ever lived."

The majority of the House did *not* favor war. Then Henry spoke. Early in his speech he made his feelings clear. "For my own part," he said, "I consider it nothing less than a question of freedom or slavery. . . There is no retreat but in submission and slavery!. . . The war is inevitable, and let it come! I repeat it,. . . let it come!. . . Gentlemen may cry Peace, but there is no peace."

His voice must have risen louder at that point. Filled with fire, Patrick Henry exclaimed, "Why stand we here idle?. . . Is life so dear, or peace so sweet, as to be purchased at the price of chains and slavery?. . . I know not what course others may take, but as for me, GIVE ME LIBERTY OR GIVE ME DEATH!"*

Reports say that all the statesmen jumped to their feet. "To arms! To arms!" they shouted. Many historians believe that Patrick Henry's powerful words launched the Revolutionary War.

---

* There was no original written text of Patrick Henry's call to arms. He spoke without notes. The speech first appeared in print in an 1817 biography of Patrick Henry.

Reflect: **Think about Patrick Henry and the American Revolution.**

1. Which of the following words describe Patrick Henry?

    orator   Virginian

    patriot traitor

    coward   Englishman

    slave   attorney

    colonist accountant

2. Complete the following sentences:

    • In the American Revolution, colonists were fighting for _____

    _____

    • As a result of the American Revolution, _____

    _____

    _____

    _____

LESSON 27: WORDS FROM HISTORY: *GIVE ME LIBERTY* . . .

RESPOND: *Circle a letter or word, fill in the blanks, or write out the answer.*

Identify a main idea.

1. Patrick Henry's famous speech could best be described as a
   a. plea for peace.
   b. call to arms.
   c. warning to the enemy.

Recall details.

2. When did Patrick Henry give this famous speech?
   _____

3. Why had the lawmakers gathered?
   _____
   _____

4. Before Henry's speech, what did most of the lawmakers there want to do?
   _____

5. What did Henry persuade them to do?
   _____

6. What did Patrick Henry say he would choose rather than give up his freedom?
   _____

Draw a conclusion.

7. Patrick Henry talked about freedom and slavery. Who did he think was enslaving the colonists?
   _____

8. We can't be sure these are Patrick Henry's exact words. Why?
   _____
   _____

Build your vocabulary.

9. Another word for *debate* is (argument / election).

10. A *statesman* is a person who is (wise in the ways of government / trained for battle).

11. An *orator* (rides horses / makes speeches).

12. The *majority* is the (greatest / smallest) part of a group.

13. *Submission* is the act of (standing up and making war / giving up and obeying).

Make a comparison.

14. Patrick Henry was a famous speech-maker. Name another famous speech-maker from American history. Tell what subject this orator most often talked about.
    _____
    _____

Look it up in a reference source.

15. Which of the following people were alive during the American Revolution?

George Washington	Betsy Ross
Abraham Lincoln	Crispus Attucks
Patrick Henry	George W. Bush
Hillary Clinton	Paul Revere
Martin Luther King, Jr.	Robert E. Lee
Benjamin Franklin	John Hancock

READ•REFLECT•RESPOND 59

READ · REFLECT · RESPOND
SUPER LESSON

READ: *Imagine crossing the country without cars or roads!*

THE OREGON TRAIL

THE ROUTE WEST

A family of emigrants stands beside a wagon near the town of Independence, Missouri. As these pioneers face the setting sun, they look west toward a new life. They are about to set off on the Oregon Trail.

The Oregon Trail was among the most famous routes leading toward America's frontier. From Independence, it wound 2,000 miles to the Pacific Northwest. In the early 1840s, word had spread about a fertile valley in that area. Government agents offered cheap farmland to those who would move there. They believed that American settlers would strengthen the United States' claim to the Oregon Territory.

Each spring, Independence, Missouri turned into a "jumping-off city." Independence boomed, filling with emigrants preparing to hit the trail. Outside of town, the prairie was packed with wagons. The pioneers set up camps and waited for the grass to grow. Why? Their animals would need to graze along the trail. By late April, the grass was high and the journey began.

A traffic jam was created as farm wagons vied for a place on the trail. Oxen and mules tangled in their lines. (Horses seldom pulled the wagons. They couldn't live off prairie grasses as well as oxen and mules.) Overpacking was a common mistake. But the inexperienced travelers soon realized that their teams couldn't pull such heavy loads. Then the first miles of the Oregon Trail were littered with household goods. The journey west took five to six months. The pioneers' goal was to reach Oregon before the first snowfall in the mountains. Travel was slow, grueling, and dangerous. In some places, emigrants faced flooding rivers. In others, they suffered drought. It is estimated that about 34,000 people died on the route. But in spite of diseases and hardships, most survived. Historians believe that between 1840 and 1860, some 300,000 emigrants traveled the Oregon Trail.

On the other side of the Rocky Mountains, near Fort Bridger, Wyoming, the route west split. Some wagons left the Oregon Trail there and went southwest along the California Trail. Others continued northwest to Oregon Territory.

The Oregon Trail passed through Missouri, Kansas, Nebraska, Wyoming, Idaho, and Oregon.

THE END OF THE TRAIL

The Grande Ronde Valley was one of the first places that greeted newcomers to Oregon. The sight of lush, green land surely filled them with relief. The emigrants would usually rest for a few days and then proceed over the Blue Mountains to The Dalles on the Columbia River. At this point, there were two ways to continue. One way was to float down the Columbia River—but this was treacherous. Some emigrants got Native Americans to take them through the rapids. Others hired professional boatmen—at a *very* high price—to ferry them westward.

Then a man named Sam Barlow came up with a plan. He'd build a road from The Dalles to the Willamette Valley. By 1846, Barlow's amazing road was finished. It wound through thick forests and crossed lofty Mount Hood. At Barlow Gate, travelers paid a toll of $5.00 per wagon. It was a tough passage. The steep slopes were almost too much for people and animals. Still, most emigrants chose the land route. That was much less frightening than facing the raging rapids of the mighty Columbia River.

Finally, the trail led to Oregon City. Many emigrants were happy to reach a town with churches, shops, mills, and even a newspaper. Some settled right there in Oregon City. They built homes and opened businesses. The rest chose to go off in different directions. The government granted each family 640 acres of Willamette Valley farmland. There, at the end of their trail, settlers staked claims, planted crops, and started to build new lives.

REFLECT: *Think about those who traveled west on the Oregon Trail.*

1. From what you know, what were some reasons that Americans moved west?

2. What hardships and dangers do you think pioneers must have faced along the trail? (List at least three.)
   -
   -
   -

3. Imagine the diary of a teenager traveling the Oregon Trail in 1842. Write one or two sentences that could appear in the diary.

4. If you'd lived in the 1840s, do you think you would have set out on the Oregon Trail? Why or why not?

Super Lesson: THE OREGON TRAIL

Respond: Circle a letter or word, fill in the blanks, or write out the answer.

Identify a main idea.

1. Which sentence presents the main idea of the reading?
   a. The Oregon Territory was a beautiful, fertile land.
   b. In the 1840s, the Oregon Trail took emigrants to new lives in the Pacific Northwest.
   c. Sam Barlow played an important role in Oregon's history.

Recall details.

2. What route took travelers into the Pacific Northwest?
   a. the California Trail
   b. Independence Road
   c. the Oregon Trail

3. Who encouraged the Americans to settle the Oregon Territory?
   a. the U.S. government
   b. bankers in Missouri
   c. Native Americans

4. What were the settlers offered?
   a. farm animals
   b. farmland
   c. cash and loans

5. What animals pulled most of the pioneer wagons?
   a. oxen and mules
   b. horses
   c. buffalo and ponies

6. When the westward route split, those who didn't follow the Oregon Trail took what route?
   a. the Santa Fe Trail
   b. the Columbia River
   c. the California Trail

7. What did travelers have to do in order to use the Barlow Road?
   a. give up some of their land
   b. pay a toll
   c. leave their belongings behind

8. About how long was the Oregon Trail?
   a. 200 feet
   b. 200 miles
   c. 2,000 miles

9. About how many pioneers are thought to have traveled the Oregon Trail?
   a. 300
   b. 3,000
   c. 300,000

Put events in order.

10. Number the following events in time-order sequence. Use information in the reading and on the maps.

    ___ Travelers reached Grande Ronde Valley.

    ___ Emigrants camped at Independence, Missouri.

    ___ Pioneers followed the Oregon Trail across the Rockies.

    ___ Pioneers crossed Mount Hood on the Barlow Road.

    ___ Some settlers stayed in Oregon City.

    ___ When the grass was high, wagons pulled out onto the Oregon Trail.

Build your vocabulary.

| emigrants | migrate | graze |
| grueling | drought | fertile |

11. To move from one place to make a new home in another place is to _____.

12. _____ are people who leave one region and settle in another.

13. A _____ is a long dry spell.

14. To _____ is to feed on growing grass.

15. A _____ journey is one that is very hard and tiring.

16. _____ land is rich enough to grow many crops.

Draw conclusions.

17. Why was Independence, Missouri, called a "jumping-off" city?

18. Why were newcomers to Oregon happy with their first sight of the Grande Ronde Valley?

19. Why did many pioneers choose to travel the Barlow Road rather than the Columbia River?

20. Why was the Barlow Road difficult to travel?

21. Why did some settlers stay in Oregon City?

22. Why did the U.S. government want Americans to settle in Oregon?

Look it up in a reference source.

23. Write three facts about the *Gila Trail*.

    • _____
    • _____
    • _____

SADDLEBACK EDUCATIONAL PUBLISHING

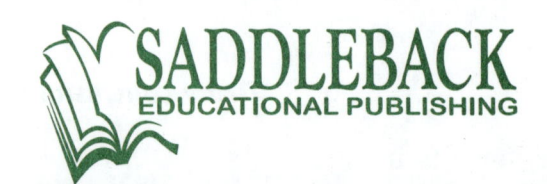

MORE EXCITING TITLES

SADDLEBACK'S "IN CONTEXT" SERIES
(Six 112-page worktexts in each series)
- English
- Vocabulary
- Reading
- Practical Math

SADDLEBACK'S "SKILLS AND STRATEGIES" SERIES
(Six 144-page reproducible workbooks in each series)
- Building Vocabulary
- Language Arts
- Math Computation
- Reading Comprehension

READING COMPREHENSION SKILL BOOSTERS
- Read-Reflect-Respond, Books A, B, C, & D

WRITING 4
(Four 64-page worktexts)
- Descriptive Writing
- Expository Writing
- Narrative Writing
- Persuasive Writing

CURRICULUM BINDERS
(100+ activities in each binder)

ENGLISH, READING, WRITING . . .
- Beginning Writing 1 & 2
- Writing 1 & 2
- Good Grammar
- Language Arts 1 & 2
- Reading for Information 1 & 2
- Reading Comprehension 1 & 2
- Spelling Steps 1, 2, 3, & 4
- Survival Vocabulary 1 & 2

MATHEMATICS . . .
- Pre-Algebra
- Algebra 1 & 2
- Geometry

SCIENCE . . .
- Earth, Life, & Physical

STUDY SKILLS & TEST PREP . . .
- Standardized Test Prep 1 & 2
- Study Skills 1 & 2

SADDLEBACK'S HIGH-INTEREST READING SERIES
- Astonishing Headlines
- Barclay Family Adventures
- Carter High
- Disasters
- Illustrated Classics Series
- Life of…Series
- PageTurners
- Quickreads
- Strange But True Stories
- Saddleback's Classics
- Walker High

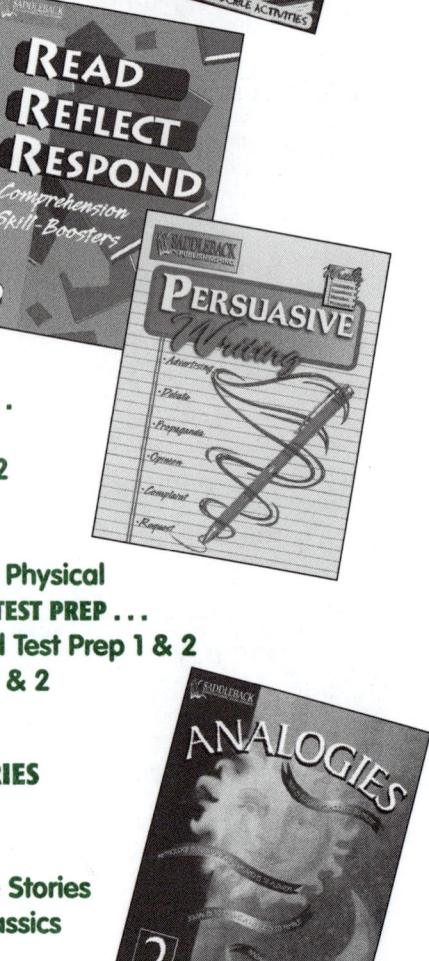

Visit us at www.sdlback.com for even more Saddleback titles.